D1117060

Prints from the art collection of
Price Development Company and Affiliates

DEPRESSION PRINTMAKERS AS WORKERS
RE-DEFINING TRADITIONAL INTERPRETATIONS

by
Mary Francey

Utah Museum of Fine Arts
University of Utah

Cover:

Wood engraving detail from

LEON GILMOUR
Cement Finishers, 1939

ACKNOWLEDGEMENTS

INITIAL WORK toward preparation of this catalog and exhibition was made possible by a 1987 summer research grant awarded by the University of Utah Research Committee. This same body further supported the work with a subsequent, and larger, grant awarded in November, 1987. This assistance is gratefully acknowledged and most sincerely appreciated.

Belief in the validity of this project was demonstrated by a third generous and very welcome research grant awarded by Robert S. Olpin, Dean of the College of Fine Arts, who has never wavered in his enthusiastic support of my interest in art of the 1930's and its impact on subsequent artistic development. Such support from an administrator who is also colleague and friend is particularly valued.

Support in the form of time and dedication to the project came from two responsible and thorough art history graduate student research assistants, Glenda Cotter and Valerie Kidrick. Letters, telephone calls and interlibrary loan procedures consumed much of their time which was always freely and cheerfully given. Each worked on a separate list of artists represented in the exhibition, gathering relevant information and writing preliminary descriptive essays which, in final form, accompany the reproductions in the catalog. Specifically, Glenda Cotter did major work on Clare Leighton, John Steuart Curry, Paul Landacre, Grant Wood, Bernard Steffen and Reginald Marsh. Valerie Kidrick was responsible for the important initial work on Henry Billings, Samuel Margolies, Leon Gilmour, Herschel Levit, Joe Jones and Irwin Hoffman. I am especially grateful to Scott Mooy, who has been involved with this project since its inception, and who is reponsible for design of the catalog. He met with us weekly, contributing valuable professional insights and imposing necessary deadlines. The commitment to this project demonstrated by these three students deserves particular mention, and has earned my heartfelt thanks.

Sincere appreciation is extended to Jennifer Bauman, Cora deJong and Barbara Ostler who contributed their interest and assistance in a seminar designed to explore the potential of this topic. Their participation in discussions and preliminary research topics helped establish a valuable body of material in preparation for the research.

Genuine thanks and sincere gratitude go to Professor Joseph Marotta for his professional assistance in documenting the exhibition. Professor Marotta photographed all prints selected for exhibition, then developed and printed those used for the catalog reproductions. His expertise is responsible for the unusually high quality of the reproductions.

Mark Petersen, Utah Museum of Fine Arts registrar, deserves particular commendation for his help with transporting and photographing the objects. Without his sense of humor and composure during minor crises, several incidents would have escalated to become problems. Sincere thanks are extended to E. Frank Sanguinetti, Director, Utah Museum of Fine Arts, for his enthusiastic suggestion that this project should be pursued, and for his assistance and guidance as the catalog evolved. I am especially indebted to Charles Loving, the museum's Assistant Director, for his willing help and for making museum resources available to me.

Appreciation is extended to Adele Lozowick for her prompt and gracious responses to my questions, and for communicating my interests to Sylvan Cole who has been an exceptionally valuable resource. The contributions of Lou Barlow and Harry Gottlieb cannot go unmentioned. Both artists were willing to discuss their Federal Art Project experiences with me, and both gave me more precise information about their individual artistic purposes. Thanks, too, to Clare Leighton for responding promptly to our questions.

In particular, I wish to thank John and Marcia Price for making their splendid collection available for study and exhibition. They have provided me with an opportunity, rare in Utah, to work with significant examples of work by major artists during a rich period in American history. Their generosity is gratefully acknowledged, and their cooperation deeply appreciated. It has been a great pleasure, also, to work with Marlene Luke of the Price Development Company and Affiliates who has been helpful, kind and understanding throughout this project.

Last, but by no means least, I wish to express thanks to Professor Sheila Muller for her continuing interest in this project, valuable critical comments, stimulating discussions and genuine collegial support.

M. F.

A SIGNIFICANT ASPECT of collecting in the United States in the past 50 years is the building of art collections by business firms. These collections are of a wide range in respect to subject matter, focus, medium, quantity and quality. And there are, literally, hundreds of such collections developed and owned by American business institutions. They are a valuable resource for the public, as most are on appropriate display, and several have been turned over to public institutions.

We know that the motives for the development of these collections by business firms are various and mixed. Some were put together to provide agreeable conditions in which to work; others enjoyed the prestige attached to important collections; others were stimulated by the special interest of owners or executives. There is good reason to believe that all were sensitive to a general awareness of the value of art in recording and stimulating desirable values.

Price Development Company and Affiliates, through the interest and leadership of John and Marcia Price, have assembled a collection of American prints which focus on the period connected with the Great Depression and after, and which give us artists' insights into the condition of the American worker of the time. It was a most interesting period for American labor and it provided conditions which set the ground for later solidarity of aims and the understanding of the contributions of the worker to the basic well-being of this country. The Price Development Company collection also, and not incidentally, gives the viewer a valuable overview of American art itself of the period.

We are indeed grateful to Mr. and Mrs. Price for the generous use of their collection for the purposes of this exhibition, and for the unusual opportunity the collection has provided for a group of students, under the direction of Professor Mary Francey of the Department of Art, to study the prints, the artists, and the general artistic and social conditions in which the prints were created. Professor Francey has contributed a fine essay which allows many insights stimulated by working closely with the collection. We are very grateful for her guest curatorship of the exhibition, as we are to the students who worked with her.

We know that the exhibition, and the catalog for which Mr. and Mrs. Price have provided the funds, will be a source of learning and enjoyment. The showing of the collection is an affirmation of the goals of the Museum and of the University.

Frank Sanguinetti, Director
Utah Museum of Fine Arts,
University of Utah
Adjunct Professor

Preceding page:

Wood engraving detail from

LOU BARLOW
Tenant Farmers, 1936

DEPRESSION PRINTMAKERS AS WORKERS RE-DEFINING TRADITIONAL INTERPRETATIONS

DURING THE 1930'S AMERICAN PRINTMAKERS abruptly but confidently divested themselves of encumbering craft traditions inherited from the past as they initiated a sequence of vigorous efforts to establish themselves as singular artists exploring various technologies of visual expression. Realizing an unprecedented sense of purpose when the United States government acknowledged the value of artistic endeavor by including artists among those unemployed workers who could apply for support by the Works Projects Administration Federal Art Project, printmakers energetically broke out of repressive and limiting artistic precedents to create a vital new print vocabulary. By producing high quality multiple originals for the purpose of creating a relevant contemporary art which was also democratic in nature, graphic artists of the 1930's brought a timely end to the use of printmaking as a means of merely reproducing paintings to illustrate inexpensive, widely distributed publications. The familiar theme "art for the people" is usually associated with murals painted for public buildings during the depression, yet depression prints were more democratic and socially conscious in theme, purpose and distribution.

While the social nature of art produced during the thirties has been extensively surveyed, comparatively little scholarship has informed original expressions by individual artists, particularly printmakers. Government welfare and relief agencies which administered programs designed to assist unemployed workers, including needy artists, recognized the practical and inexpensive aspects of prints as accordant with the stated Federal Art Project purpose of making original works of art accessible to a wide viewing audience. Visual interpretations of social and political conditions in prints of this period are especially pertinent reactions by artists to the immediate, troubled environment which was experienced to some extent by the entire population of the country, but most profoundly by the middle-class majority. Prints were obviously better able to communicate visual confirmation of middle class experience to a large and aesthetically unsophisticated viewing public than paintings which, in comparison, achieved limited exposure. It is historically significant to the study of American art history that prints and printmaking during the thirties assumed a well deserved status equal to that of painting and sculpture, including the requisite conditions of originality and creativity.

Equally significant are the unique contributions to printmaking made by artists working in groups in graphic arts workshops, particularly those who investigated new print processes which became pivotal innovations, establishing major new directions of development. These creative explorations account for the integration of printmaking into the work of major artists of the 1960's, including Andy Warhol, Robert Rauschenberg, Frank Stella and Robert Motherwell, for without the establishment of a silk screen workshop within the New York Graphic Arts Division of the Federal Art Project it is unlikely that the screen print would so quickly have become accepted as a fine art technique. Experimental, too, was the incorporation of expressive use of color in lithography and woodcut. Most artists involved in Project workshops had travelled and studied in Europe and were familiar with contemporary German woodcuts which directly connected Jugenstil symbolism with the exaggerated overstatements of expressionist social protest. Many, including Benton Spruance, Louis Lozowick and Reginald Marsh, had also worked at the Atelier Desjobert in Paris where they were introduced to the intricacies of the two-color lithograph. Both processes had previously been used chiefly as commercial techniques for reproducing paintings and were assigned, therefore, the less prestigious status of craft.

Although there is a large existing, and continually expanding, body of scholarship which informs American painting, both easel and mural, produced under the auspices of the Federal Art Project between its inception in August 1935 and final dissolution in June 1943, comparatively little research has been devoted specifically to individual printmakers and their unique purposes during that period. In fact, graphic arts divisions were important facets of the Federal Art Project, and were responsible for supporting and encouraging printmakers who enthusiastically originated more than 6,000 designs for nearly 100,000 prints for allocation to public buildings. These included lithographs, wood engravings, wood block prints and etchings in black and white, as well as experimental procedures in color etching, lithography and woodcut. Decidedly as important was the inauguration, within the New York graphics workshop, of the silk screen method as a fine art process. Like Project painters and sculptors, printmakers included artists with established reputations as well as others who were, and remain, virtually unknown. The recent resurgence of interest in, and reassessment of, art of the thirties consequently emphasizes the need to devote more research to printmakers who made significant contributions then, but whose names have become unfamiliar.

Establishment of graphic arts divisions within the Federal Art Project in 1935 raised hopes that those visual artists who were drawn to printmaking as a primary method of expression would have opportunities previously reserved almost exclusively for painters and sculptors. Printmakers, who previously had a limited market, and consequently a limited audience, now became members of the larger community of artists originating works for a public whose support they could rely upon. Furthermore, Project workshops offered opportunities for exploring techniques previously prohibited by cost of equipment and lack of adequate space. Workshops provided facilities which included high quality presses and skilled master printers for artists who often worked in cooperative groups, exchanging ideas and offering each other critical appraisals of evolving works. The workshops fostered a sense of mutually supportive community which effectively nurtured embryonic individual styles. However, apart from original prints by such major early twentieth-century figures as Joseph Pennell, John Sloan, and Stuart Davis, there was little in the way of an important printmaking tradition for Project artists to inherit or, for that matter, to react against. Although technical competence was emphasized, originality had not been encouraged, a condition which had kept American printmaking from becoming anything but an ineffective imitation of previous styles. Earlier American artists had, of course, developed strong reputations in etching, but their success was largely due to close adherence to European methods which had been tenaciously perpetuated by American print societies. Commercial lithographers, including Currier and Ives, had identified the popular and widely marketed chromolithographs as mass-produced images which offered familiar, nostalgic themes rendered in meticulous detail, and which were intended to appeal directly to the conventional level of aesthetic understanding of the American public. Modern painting styles furnished some degree of guidance in possible imaginative directions printmakers might investigate, but most of these could not effectively record diverse social and humanitarian themes dictated by prevailing economic conditions. The challenge for the American printmaker of the thirties was in the need to search for unique individual expressions, relevant to current social circumstances, which could also be apprehended, interpreted and appreciated by the general public. Printmakers not only met the challenge, but were responsible for developing innovative procedures which led directly to radical and influential changes in print vocabulary.

Although the country's consciousness had not yet been systematically raised with respect to the role of women and minorities in society, let alone in art, women and blacks were prominent members of Federal Art Project workshops. A large number of women are listed in records of graphic art divisions, including Wanda Gag, Mabel Dwight, Elizabeth Olds, all assigned to the New York Project, and Mary Huntoon who worked with the Project in Topeka, Kansas. Because of the opportunities offered by graphic workshops, women printmakers were among those who established important precedents for subsequent artistic development.

For example, when Olds insisted elitist art was no longer appropriate in view of current social concerns and that art should be brought closer to the public, she unknowingly predicted later artistic intentions of narrowing the gap between art and life which characterized much work of the 1960's and 70's. Women, too, concentrated on searching out personal iconographies to describe their reactions to current conditions. It is of particular interest to note that 40% of those identified as practicing professionals in art in 1930 were women, and of the artists receiving assistance under the Federal Art Project between 1936 and 1940, 40% also were women. This indicates that women were acknowledged as competent artists who were obviously capable of functioning in a historically male dominated profession. Furthermore, Project committees did not demonstrate gender bias when selecting from among a pool of applicants, a fact which may be due to the large number of female Project administrators.[1] Although women working in offices and factories were often required to yield their jobs to unemployed men, there is no evidence that women artists on the Project experienced similar expulsion from their chosen vocation. Like their male counterparts, women printmakers such as Isabel Bishop searched for socially relevant themes among lower and middle class women struggling to preserve the social advances toward individual rights they had made during the 1920's.

Included in this exhibition are *Merry Go Round* (1940), *Modern 1939 Venus* (1939), and *Chop Suey Dancers* (1930), all by Reginald Marsh, and which depict the dilemma experienced by women during the depression. These ample females who do not work, and who are overtly sensual yet remote and unattainable, are not willing to relinquish their recently established social identities, yet there is little hope of gainful employment with which to sustain their precious newly won independence. Not all, however, have abandoned their traditional roles. The busy housewife in Harry Gottlieb's *Going to Work* (1940) has just finished hanging her laundry out to dry in an environment polluted by factory smoke, and is propping the clothes-line to prevent the heavy, wet garments from sagging to the ground. This resolute woman and many like her, joined by Marsh's buxom young broads, will soon, as the second World War erupts, also go off to factory jobs to fill vacancies created as men leave for military service.

Racism, too, was virtually non-existent on the Federal Art Project, although there is some evidence of inequities which will be discussed later in this essay. Recognized as thoroughly capable participants in all Project assignments, black artists happily abandoned past naive and saccharine styles in favor of forceful, eloquent images which were more appropriate to black cultural concerns during the Depression. The general consciousness of a need to improve race relations resulted in expanded art education opportunities in southern states, and in an encouragement of artistic production in northern cities, including New York and Philadelphia.[2] The Harlem Community Art Center in New York City also included classes for children in simple and inexpensive woodcut and linoleum block processes. Samuel Joseph Brown, also a painter and teacher, produced linoleum cuts under the Federal Art Project, and Dox Thrash, employed as a printer in the Philadelphia graphics workshop, is credited with initiating the experiments which led to invention of the carborundum process. When carborundum etchings, which are unusually rich in tone and luminosity, were first exhibited in Washington, D.C. in 1938, they elicited widespread interest because of the potential for individuation during inking of the plate.

Development of those unique, innovative styles which emerged during the Depression within the context of socially conscious art has often been attributed to the welfare programs which allowed artists to work freely without having to concern themselves with marketing their work. Another explanation however may be the as yet unresolved and generally unspoken, but compelling, need felt by American artists to establish a direction independent of European tradition. Uncomfortable with aesthetic theories and reluctant to investigate abstraction in its various emerging forms, a substantial number of Project artists found sources for individual expression in the impact on humanity of political and social effects of the Depression. In part this took the form of the social realism as expressed by the messages in paintings by Ben Shahn, photographs of devastating effects of the drought on migrant workers by Dorothea Lange, and protest in murals by Diego Rivera, Jose Orozco and David Siquieros, among many others who made strong pictorial responses to the effect on society of the current national crisis. Another, and less familiar, development emphasized the individual in contrast to the social realist purpose of commenting on group experience, and seemed to call attention to the importance of each human being engaged in productive labor. It is in the assertion of the worth and contributions of the individual worker that artists of the thirties often found validation of their own efforts and purposes. This was particularly true in the case of printmakers who were assigned to government sponsored workshops in which they had the freedom to explore technical innovations as well as individual directions of professional development within a community of other artists with similar intentions.

Holger Cahill, National Director of the Federal Art Project, observed in 1938 that it would be possible to reconstruct a visual history of the period of the Depression from prints created by artists on the Project.[3] Inasmuch as the history of the Depression is closely integrated with the history of labor in the United States, a condition which is reflected in prints of the time, Cahill's statement was justified. Because they developed a strong interest in the point of view of the laborer, both employed and unemployed, printmakers created some of the most eloquent visual descriptions of cultural responses to the Depression by rural and urban working America. Furthermore, artists were categorized, in the minds of Project administrators, as unemployed workers in need of federal assistance. Inevitably, the identities of artists became so closely associated with the workers they portrayed that many figures in prints produced during the Depression may not be anonymous laborers after all, but might more accurately be interpreted as representations of artists assuming the roles of the workers portrayed. It may, therefore, be time to re-examine the persistent myth of the social realist artist of the Depression depicting anonymous, muscular figures based on a conventionalized visual form, as dehumanized victims of industry. Further inquiry might also serve to modify a corresponding myth that suggests images of busy industrial workers are most accurately interpreted as symbols of optimism during a period of social and economic crisis.

To assume that the body of work produced under sponsorship of the Project was primarily social/democratic in nature as well as purpose is to deny both the presence and responsibility of the artists, particularly printmakers, who identified closely with the circumstances of workers during the Depression. The familiar laborer who so often appears in prints and paintings of the thirties is a muscular figure typically pictured as either integrating convincingly with, or exerting an intellectual control over, the machines and tools with which he works. Inevitably many Project printmakers developed a particular interest in depicting the point of view of people to whom work was a fundamental objective in itself. Obviously workers wanted, and deserved, fair compensation for their efforts, but additional important motivations were the rewards intrinsic to work as a process. Printmaker and laborer both shared a sense of purpose which had its origins in the sense of satisfaction each derived from working at their professions

ARTISTIC
PURPOSES
REVISED

13

of choice. The nature of both medium and process render printmaking the most democratic and aesthetically educational endeavor of any of the creative arts supported by the Federal Art Project. Prints represent the ideal integration of artist with craftsman and, simultaneously, involved both process and product more directly with the public.

Government support for the arts gave artists in general a sense of self esteem and social status which contrasted perceptibly with public understanding of the role of artists in society during earlier periods in American history. American viewers were traditionally inclined to regard the fine arts as elitist, precious and difficult to comprehend, an impression which had long isolated artists from the public. Americans in general had historically equated the visual arts with luxury and saw them as the prerogative of upper classes only. Even worse, art was associated with European aristocratic and religious attitudes and thus inconsistent with democratic ideals. A statement in the Prospectus of the People's Art Guild of 1915 observed that artists and people were following divergent directions, and both were losing in the resultant separation. The same document noted that people's aesthetic deprivation was as complete as the isolation felt by artists. Due largely to the decidedly conventional level of art critical perception in this country, artists who had previously attempted genuine response to their surroundings, as Arthur B. Davies, Marsden Hartley, John Marin and other modernists had done, were not widely acknowledged. It was not until the federal government recognized the worth of artistic activity by including artists among the vast numbers of unemployed who could apply for assistance during the Depression that American artists finally attained the sense of social endorsement for which they had so long yearned. "Art is a normal social growth rooted deeply in the life of mankind and extremely sensitive to environments created by human society," wrote Holger Cahill in his catalog introduction for the 1936 exhibition *New Horizons in American Art*, a visual survey of one year's activity on the Federal Art Project.[4] He went on to note that art cannot be kept alive by a few artists so committed they are willing to endure social and physical deprivation; their survival depends upon patronage.[5] Cahill often invoked John Dewey's philosophy to substantiate the argument that art, as the most civilized means of communication, provides an efficient means of entering sympathetically into the most profound life experiences of all people.

But patronage inevitably imposes conditions to which its recipients are expected to conform. Although the primary intent of the Federal Art Project was more correctly included within the massive New Deal effort to create work relief programs designed to revive the faltering economy, and not exclusively to patronize the arts, still it established specific criteria which artists were required to meet. Like other unemployed workers, artists were required to make formal application for federal assistance, and only those who qualified were eligible for assignments to various mural, easel, photography, graphic arts and sculpture projects. Project goals included incorporating the arts within the daily life of the community in general, a purpose which supported the larger attempt to achieve an integration of the fine and practical arts. The cooperative and democratic nature of prints and printmaking processes was consistent with such goals, and held out the promise that a more democratic expression would be accessible to a large viewing public, thereby helping to "heal the breach between artist and public that has become distressingly evident in the contemporary period."[6] Elizabeth Olds, a Project artist from 1935 until 1940, wrote that at least one of the purposes of the New York graphic arts division was to enable artists to produce prints in sufficient quantities that original works of art could be introduced to "every man, woman and child in America to enjoy art on a wide popular basis."[7] Noting that culturally illiterate Americans needed to learn the language of art, Olds advocated making the availability of art comparable to the free public school system. She held that new uses for, and applications of, graphic art should be explored at regional community levels to acquaint people with art as a necessary aspect of their lives.

DIVIDED INTO FOUR MAJOR DIVISIONS: mural, easel, sculpture, and graphic arts, the Federal Art Project employed 5,300 artists during its peak year of 1936. In June of that year a total of 3,650 artists, 70% of whom were men and 30% women, were employed. The 50 printmakers assigned to the New York City graphics arts workshop alone created more than 75,000 etchings, lithographs, wood engravings and screen prints for distribution to various public institutions. Initiated in August 1935, the graphics divisions, nationwide, had allocated their entire output to a total of 13,458 tax-supported municipal, state, and federal institutions by June 1940. The Project employed 250 printmakers assigned to sixteen graphic divisions, including those particularly productive workshops in New York, California, Michigan, Florida, Ohio, Maryland, Connecticut and Pennsylvania.

The success of the graphic arts division in New York was largely due to Audrey McMahon's recognition of the potential of printmaking as an efficient and inexpensive means of creating original works of art in sufficiently large quantities that their apportionment would be far more widespread than could be expected from paintings. McMahon was director of the New York region of the Federal Art Project for the duration of its existence, and has been credited with possession of the aesthetic understanding and vision necessary to ensure success for the project while allowing artists to retain a sense of dignity and self worth in spite of the conviction of the local WPA administrator, Colonel Brehon Somerville, that artists were social parasites incapable of serious work, and should not be allowed to obtain federal support.[8] Acting on the advice of Bernarda Bryson (Mrs. Ben Shahn), McMahon appointed Russell Limbach, an experienced printer and well-known artist, to plan and organize the central graphic arts workshop. He was also charged with design of the printing shop, procurement of necessary equipment and supplies, as well as recruiting skilled printers. Equipment, obviously, included various presses, the cost of which was not covered by federal funds, necessitating solicitations from private donors. When the New York studio workshop for graphic artists was officially opened on February 6, 1936, it offered a well-equipped facility for producing etchings, lithographs, wood block prints and wood engravings under the general direction of Gustave von Groschwitz who had been appointed supervisor of the graphic arts division, with Russell Limbach as technical adviser and Theodore Wahl as shop chairman. Wahl did most of the lithographic printing and, during 1938, Augustus Peck acted as shop chairman of the etching department. During the first few months of its existence, 61 artists were assigned to the workshop, and were provided with materials for making prints and drawings suitable for allocation to qualifying institutions. Recipients of these works were asked for modest donations calculated to cover costs of materials, thereby rendering the print project partially self-supporting.

More transportable and less intimidating than paintings, prints were identified by Project supervisory staff as the logical popular medium for the public. Inasmuch as etchings, lithographs and wood engravings were typically printed in editions of 25 to 50 impressions of each image, it was obvious that more prints than paintings could be made available to appropriate institutions to be seen daily by a wide segment of the viewing public. It is, unfortunately, also true that distribution on so large a scale resulted in a general tendency to consider prints as less valuable than painting, which has been posited as one explanation for the official neglect which might account for the disappearance of so many works by artists who have since become critically acclaimed. For example, only twelve of the lithographs which Jackson Pollock produced, and Theodore Wahl printed, between 1934 and 1937 are extant.

Before beginning a print, each artist was required to submit a drawing to both the Project supervisor and a supervising artist such as Carl Zigrosser (curator of prints at the Philadelphia Museum of Art) in order to ensure the theme was appropriate (although subject matter was rarely censored) and that the print was of acceptable artistic quality. At the time of proofing, artists would collaborate with printer and supervisor until the image was considered satisfactory, then six proofs were submitted to a committee of project supervisors for final approval. It can be assumed, therefore, that many of the prints produced under sponsorship of the graphic arts division reflect the critical standards of project supervisors as well as intentions of the artists who created them. However, there is little evidence that changes other than occasional modifications in technical process were requested.

The most creative period of the graphic arts divisions can be dated 1937–38 when technical processes were expanded to include color printing. Color lithography, under the supervision of Russell Limbach as technical adviser, was initiated early in 1937, and resulted in inclusion of 23 color lithographs in the 1938 exhibition, *Printmaking, A New Tradition* at the Fifty-Seventh Street Federal Gallery. Limbach had worked in color since 1930 in spite of the prevailing opinion that chromolithography was a technique suitable only for reproducing paintings, and, therefore, not appropriate for the production of original prints. After 1938, however, color lithographs which incorporated as many as five colors, were successfully printed by graphic arts workshops and were of such high quality that they were in more demand than black and white impressions. This remarkable achievement owes its success to the costly equipment provided by the government-sponsored workshop, and the equally costly skills of such master printers as Jacob Friedland, George Miller and Theodore Wahl, as well as the enthusiastic encouragement of Limbach and his supervisor, Gustave von Groschwitz.

A screen printing unit, established in 1938, was headed by Anthony Velonis who had worked in commercial studios and for the Project's poster division. The increasing popularity of color lithographs had succeeded in enticing artists into the realm of color printing, but the expensive equipment necessary made lithography accessible to only a few. Less expensive and more fluent, screen printing appealed to such pioneers as Harry Gottlieb and Louis Lozowick, both of whom are represented in this exhibition. Velonis authored two handbooks describing the process which were mimeographed by the Federal Art Project and eagerly acquired by Project and private artists nationwide. Because it needed only simple, inexpensive equipment, screen printing acquired immediate and widespread appeal. Furthermore, because artists did their own printing, it re-established a direct relationship between idea and process, a condition which the intervention of the master printer in etching and lithography had altered. The silk screen process was quickly designated as serigraphy by Velonis and Carl Zigrosser to distinguish it from already familiar commercial methods. Serigraphy was a combination of the Latin for silk (seri) and the Greek term for writing or drawing (graphein). Velonis worked to increase the range of effects available to printmakers, and it is primarily due to his pioneering efforts that the screen printing process has become equal in status to lithography, etching and woodcut. First explored by Project artists including Louis Lozowick, Elizabeth Olds and Ruth Chaney, it was later used by such historically familiar figures as Josef Albers, Robert Rauschenberg, Andy Warhol and Frank Stella.[9] Thus, a new color process was inaugurated which was destined to make significant impact on major movements during the 1960's and 70's.

The two screen prints by Harry Gottlieb, *Change of Shift* (1940) and *Going to Work* (1941), are examples of themes which adapted logically to this new mode of expression. At 93 years of age, Gottlieb still works regularly in his New York studio, and recalls how artists during the thirties responded to the drama of the stimulus of the Depression and the sense of community created by the Federal Art Project.[10] Gottlieb's figures, for example, are determined workers who march happily off to their jobs, clutching packed lunches, then join the line of cheerful workers entering a factory now fully operational and spewing great clouds of smoke from its tall stacks. A member of a small pilot project, Gottlieb worked enthusiastically with Velonis to investigate as thoroughly as possible the potential of the screen process. Both successful and prolific, he held the first one-man exhibition of screen prints in 1940.[11] Like his colleagues, Gottlieb concentrated on achieving a successful combination of technical possibilities with imaginative imagery, and he did so with a humility characteristic of Project artists. Although strong individual styles developed within this period, and a sense of community emerged from the need to organize to create one political voice (Gottlieb was an active member of the Artist's Union), there was little evidence of egocentrism among graphic arts division members.

Color woodcuts and engravings, too, were eagerly explored in 1938. Artists exploited the responsive grains available in large planks of gumwood or cherry, and experimented by raising the printing surface with cement and lowering it by sanding. The resulting rich prints inspired McMahon to state in her November, 1938, report to Holger Cahill that, "printmakers in the graphic arts division are opening new avenues of approach to graphic media and are also re-establishing the values of techniques that have been neglected."[12] American artists had not attempted much work in color woodcut other than producing some banalities which mimicked Japanese prints. With the encouragement of the Federal Art Project, however, artists experimented with possibilities for varying color intensities and textures.

The only color wood engraving in this exhibition, Lou Barlow's *Tenant Farmers* (1936), is not a naive regionalist expression but an observation, made by a sophisticated urban artist, of current rural conditions which were directly affecting the entire country. Taught the process by Lynd Ward while assigned to the New York graphic arts division, Barlow still works daily in his studio and deplores the fact that he cannot find the end grain wood blocks necessary for wood engravings. He has been forced to substitute linoleum block, another technique for which the necessary material is rapidly becoming scarce. The couple in *Tenant Farmers* appear to be pondering their assigned roles as workers subservient to landowners who misused both soil and people. As the drought worsened, southern sharecroppers and tenant farmers in the mid-west lost their jobs, often to be replaced by machines thought to be more efficient and less costly.[13] Exploitation of the land, now recognized as the greater environmental abuse of the 1920's and 30's, is also evident in Barlow's engraving. Farmers had for too long ignored the wisdom of crop rotation and contour plowing, demanding more from the earth than was realistic without a restorative program. Such violation of the country's natural agrarian resources forced government intervention in the form of regulatory and educational programs. Reclamation of the land became a national concern, and urban communities were kept closely informed of the devastation of the land by a growing news media. Barlow, working in New York, was made aware of the general desperation of the rural experience by photographers employed by the Farm Security Administration as well as by constant newsreel coverage.

Nourished by government patronage, Project artists acquired a collective identity, but what is far more significant, began to discover strong individual identities, intentions and styles. Printmakers, especially, realized a sense of self worth which derived directly from their unique charge to create visual images which could be reproduced for the purpose of communicating with the American public, a challenging new and untried audience for artists. Inasmuch as the public for whom prints were intended consisted of members of the work force, the identity of the printmaker inevitably aligned with that of the worker. While it is true the unemployed were measured in unprecedentedly large numbers, they were, in fact, a minority.[14] Furthermore, the standard of living in the United States was high compared with that of Europe and England, with an annual wage for industrial workers of more than $1500. In comparison, artists assigned to Project workshops earned approximately $1100 per year, emphasizing their kinship with the American worker. With the realization that their government had recognized their worth as contributing members of society, American artists developed a sense of purpose and self assurance which is immediately evident in the clear, vigorous prints which depict the experience of the worker during the Depression.

ALTHOUGH MORE APPARENT DURING THE THIRTIES, work and worker themes, both urban and rural, appeared as integral ingredients of the American print vocabulary during the early years of the twentieth century. Industrial images emerged as early as 1912 when Joseph Pennell recorded progress on the Panama Canal, observing industry on a colossal scale. As artist on the site, Pennell was permitted to move freely through the construction, creating such lucid preliminary drawings that one of the workers was convinced they "would work." Shortly after completion of this series, Pennell turned his attention to the terrifying machinery of war, making meticulous studies of munitions factories in England, France and Germany. He contrasted gun pits, furnaces and forges with sketchy, transient little figures of workers moving through and around the overpowering machinery, unable to dominate and devoid of individualism. As a Quaker, he was opposed to war; it made him so physically ill that he was rendered totally incapable of sketching while visiting the French front during the first World War where he was confronted with the harsh realities of combat. In spite of his aversion to war, Pennell had discovered a compelling inner response to the industrial character of his world, becoming completely absorbed in the "wonder of work," and declaring, "Work is the greatest thing in the world."[15]

Placed in charge of the etching class at the Art Student's League in 1922, Pennell was a demanding teacher who never permitted students to settle for the first workable image they designed, but insisted they push the plate beyond the obvious solution, searching for an original and individual result. His efforts at the League were intensified by a determination to overcome the poor work habits, lack of purpose and ignorance of art historical knowledge he observed in American students. He encouraged class discussions, accompanied students on assigned visits to museums, and constantly cautioned them to forego their persistent tendencies to imitate, reminding them that to copy is to invite comparison.[16] He also instilled in his students a strong desire to become bold and original, and to refuse to supply the market with the prevalent standardized brand of art labelled "what the people want" when, in reality, it was all they could get.[17] Pennell's teaching created a solid foundation for a new generation of printmakers who preferred not to be judged as illustrators, but as artists exploring the full innovative potential of printmaking methods.

The origins of Pennell's ineffectual figures may be found in the landscapes of the 19th century Hudson River School, many of which include the presence of man as an inconsequential element all but invisible in an overpowering romantic wilderness. These tiny figures, lost in the grandeur of an unspoiled nature, predict the devastating effect man will have upon his environment as the luminous serenity of the unexplored landscape is relentlessly obscured by the steam, smoke and bustle of heavily populated, industrialized modern spaces. Man, who intrudes tentatively on nature in mid-19th century landscapes, is the ancestor of Pennell's agitated little people who are bewildered by the scale of surrounding derricks, forges and locks which they have created but which possess a power still incomprehensible to them. From the alien human who was first dwarfed by the wilderness he entered, but who finally destroyed its equilibrium, man evolved through work into the self assured foreman in Herschel Levit's *Take It Away*, and the pneumatic

19

drill operator in Louis Lozowick's *Birth of a Skyscraper,* both of whom are absorbed in, and capable of, re-organizing nature. Lozowick is especially representative of the printmakers who identified directly with the workers they represented, evaluating their prints in terms of craft and technical competence.

Joseph Pennell's preoccupation with work as a theme is echoed in Federal Art Project prints produced during the depression. Many of the artists assigned to the New York graphics workshop had been students in his popular, heavily enrolled classes at the League. This new generation, however, was less inclined to emphasize the machine as dominant, but included figures which presented human authority as the essential element. Unlike Pennell's romantic views of industrial spaces filled with monumental machinery, printmakers during the thirties focused more logically on workers, creating visual statements about the rewards intrinsic to hard work. Workers in prints of the thirties are not subservient to the machines which inhabit their world, they integrate convincingly with, and exert control over, their factory and industrial environments. These workers now confidently manage the environment over which they have gained superiority. They are no longer dominated by either nature or machine.

In addition to the obvious need to earn a living wage, an equally important incentive during the depression was the distinct sense of purpose experienced by people who could find satisfaction in the knowledge that their labors would help create a semblance of order in a country disrupted by economic crisis. Because artists were among the large numbers of unemployed who were supported by the massive New Deal relief programs, they viewed themselves as cultural workers and were, therefore, logically allied with the concerns of labor. These included organizing into militant unions established to protect themselves against unfair hiring and firing practices by WPA committees. A major reason for these unprecedented militant practices on the part of artists was that, as a social class, they were members of the majority, and because the majority were unemployed, they were considered, in terms of class distinctions, to be "have nots." However, for American artists this was at least acknowledgement of their existence, and formed a connection with the general society from which they had historically been estranged.

There was of course a price for this official recognition and validation of art as worthy of federal support. Artists faced the open hostility of critics who were politically opposed to cultural projects, and who did not hesitate to accuse them, and the agencies which assisted them, of wasting precious tax dollars on frivolities which could demonstrate no practical result. Many local WPA supervisors were firmly convinced that making pictures could not be construed as work, and worse, art projects were suspected of encouraging the spread of Communism. In addition, supervisory methods were stringent and unrealistic, requiring Project artists to sign in at designated locations daily before 9 a.m., then return home to work for the rest of the day. They were obliged to remain at home, or their specified place of work, where they were periodically checked on, unannounced, by timekeepers. If an artist did not answer the door when a timekeeper came by (relief recipients were not permitted telephones), he or she was recorded as absent without leave. This caused hardships for artists who needed, among other things, to leave working locations occasionally to acquire materials. If an artist wanted to sketch away from home the administration required notification as to precise location, and frequently sent a timekeeper to the site to verify the artist was indeed present and working.[18] These tactics were degrading, unrealistic and clearly indicated that most WPA supervisors did not comprehend the nature of artistic activity.

Because of such demeaning stipulations, many artists with only the most meager means chose to avoid applying for relief. Others, including Jackson Pollock, were almost entirely dependent upon the Project for their livelihood, and dutifully presented themselves at their assigned locations each morning. Pollock liked to work late at night, then sleep late in the morning which made the 9 a.m. deadline especially difficult for him. He was often observed running frantically along the streets toward the time clock at his designated center, still dressed in pajamas, to sign in with only seconds to spare.[19] Failure to meet the daily deadline meant the withholding of that week's paycheck. In spite of these inconveniences, Pollock, along with most Project artists, was grateful for the aid, often recalling how it had kept him alive during a period of extreme hardship.

Even more abusive was the policy of firing, begun as early as 1936, which required project artists to be terminated every eighteen months to permit them to seek private employment. This was a particularly cruel hoax, since, obviously, the private sector held out no hope for jobs for artists. Artists were frequently accepted for work, then when funding was altered, summarily dismissed with a final payment. There were no criteria for selection of those slated for dismissal; the process was entirely random, and artists were discharged without prior notice, simply by means of a pink slip included with their paychecks. In the summer of 1937, Harry Hopkins ordered a total of 600,000 people eliminated from WPA rolls, and in 1939, forty percent of the artists assigned to the New York project received pink slips, with planned discharges for 400 more.

It was during these enforced cuts that Audrey McMahon, who had scrupulously followed a policy of racial non-discrimination, was compelled to comply with the demand made by the militant Harlem Artists' Guild that blacks be listed as blacks, and that special quotas be established for them.[21] McMahon voiced strong disagreement with this practice, preferring that dismissal decisions be made independent of race since unemployment, she reasoned, was shared by whites and blacks alike. The specter of discrimination, however, had surfaced, and blacks began to identify special concerns which set them apart as a racial minority group.

Once dismissed, it was possible to request reinstatement to the project, but in order to do so, artists had to declare themselves paupers in order to be allowed to apply for relief. To qualify for home relief, one had no choice but to submit to an investigation which determined if the applicant had property or possible means of support, however minimal, including savings or insurance, which might be converted into money. Those who qualified had to wait in relief centers every day, along with other unemployed workers and derelicts, for a job opening to be listed on the blackboard. When such a listing appeared, all too seldom (i.e., "graphic artist, WPA" with the employer's address), each artist would rush headlong for the first street car going in that direction; the first to arrive usually got the job upon presentation of a relief voucher. Among other degrading associations, the relief voucher implied its holder was unable to manage funds satisfactorily, and was desperate enough to accept any task, however humiliating, for the most meager pay. Waiting in relief centers required untold patience and tenacity, as well as an ability to resist the temptations of other job opportunities which were listed. These included "dishwasher," "porter," "general handyman," and similar jobs for persons with no special skills. An artist who accepted one of these, however, no longer qualified as a Project artist. Work for artists was often only available in remote areas such as, in one instance, a Civilian Worker Camp in a rural area where a scarlet fever epidemic was at its peak. Jackson Pollock was dismissed from the Project several times, and had no choice but to reapply for relief in spite of his brother Sanford's efforts to protect him from the humiliation of this daily ordeal.

On the other hand, any artists who participated in graphic arts projects were grateful that they could survive economically, and were enthusiastic about the opportunity to be able to work with other artists and master printers. Recognition of their unique abilities, and support to allow them to concentrate on creative endeavor were undeniably provided by the government. However, WPA administrative procedures often ran counter to any intended positive effects by placing artists in the same categories as indigent nonworkers. Some felt these indignities were compensated for by the freedom they were given to explore evolving personal styles and opportunities for having resulting images professionally printed. Proofing their blocks and stones in the company of such recognized professionals as Stuart Davis, Raphael Soyer, Adolph Dehn and Louis Lozowick was an exhilarating experience. Stimulating, too, was the continuing requirement of maintaining high levels of individual productivity as well as frequent opportunities to work within a community of like-minded colleagues who continually debated the apparently unlimited possibilities of new print processes.

Project printmakers were a transitional generation, demonstrating the expressive potential of individual artists who were officially recognized and nurtured by relief measures, but were allowed creative freedom. Individual iconographical development was made possible by a system which permitted artists to work daily knowing they would be regularly compensated for their efforts. Direct involvement with various processes, access to equipment and opportunities to interact with other Project artists, including painters, writers, musicians and actors, created a stimulating environment in which all could produce their best work. The high quality work which resulted has contributed important aesthetic legacies, not the least of which is, finally, the realization that historically and socially significant art does not have to occupy the rarefied realm of the elite object. Now art can function in the gap between art and life as a connective device between creative genius and the beholder who recreates both idea and process in which the artist engaged. Because Project printmakers naturally associated themselves and their purposes with the working middle class, they are perhaps more directly responsible than painters for eliciting the interest of the public, and thereby creating the new and wider range of supportive audiences who have become today's corporate patrons of the arts.

¹ Wendy Slatkin, *Women Artists in History* (New Jersey: Prentice-Hall, Inc. 1985), p. 115.

² William F. McDonald, *Federal Relief Administration and the Arts* (Columbus: Ohio State University Press, 1969), p. 412.

³ McDonald, p. 435.

⁴ Holger Cahill, *New Horizons in American Art* (New York: Museum of Modern Art, 1936), p. 9.

⁵ Cahill, p. 10.

⁶ Cahill, p. 21.

⁷ Elizabeth Olds, "Prints for Mass Production," in *Art For The Millions*, ed. Francis V. O'Connor (New York: New York Graphic Society, Ltd. 1973), p. 142.

⁸ Audrey McMahon, "A General View of the WPA Federal Art Project in New York City and State," in *The New Deal Art Projects—An Anthology of Memoirs*, ed. Francis V. O'Connor (Washington, D.C.: Smithsonian Institution Press, 1972), p. 63.

⁹ Christopher DeNoon, *Posters of the WPA* (Los Angeles: The Wheatley Press, 1987), p. 21.

¹⁰ One of the most rewarding experiences while working on this catalog was the opportunity to speak directly by telephone with Harry Gottlieb on January 29, 1988. Gottlieb reiterated the opinions held by most Project artists that, although poverty was a major concern, the benefits of meeting other printmakers in the context of graphic arts workshops made the late thirties a period of unusual creativity and productivity.

¹¹ New York, "New York City WPA Art," *New York City WPA Art Then 1934–43 and Now 1960–1977*, "Harry Gottlieb," p. 36.

¹² Jacob Kainen, "The Graphic Arts Division of the WPA Federal Art Project," in *The New Deal Art Projects—An Anthology of Memoirs*, p. 170.

¹³ "Landscape," *Art News*, 27, No. 2 (1983), p. 39–40.

¹⁴ John Garraty, *The Great Depression* (New York: Harcourt Brace Jovanovich, 1986), p. 86–87.

¹⁵ Elizabeth Robins Pennell, *The Life and Letters of Joseph Pennell* (Boston: Little, Brown and Co., 1929), p. 116.

¹⁶ Mary Francey, *Joseph Pennell—Illustrator and Printmaker*, Thesis, University of Utah, 1974, p. 68.

¹⁷ Francey, p. 69.

¹⁸ Kainen, p. 163.

¹⁹ Deborah Solomon, *Jackson Pollock* (New York: Simon and Schuster, Inc., 1987), p. 80.

²⁰ McMahon, p. 57.

²¹ McDonald, p. 412.

²² Solomon, p. 83.

²³ Kainen, p. 166.

NOTES

Opposite page:

Etching detail from

ISAC FRIEDLANDER
Warming Up, ca. 1935

LOU BARLOW

THE WOOD ENGRAVING at the right, *Tenant Farmers*, 1936, was printed by Lou Barlow while he was assigned to the graphic arts division of the New York City Federal Art Project. Barlow, in fact, was assigned to the Public Works of Art Project in 1933, and was continually employed as a government artist during the transition to the WPA/FAP, until he resigned in 1939. Graduating in painting and sculpture from the National Academy of Art in 1930, an idealistic Barlow and his colleagues were eager to plunge into the world of fine art, only to realize that, as the economic crisis in the country worsened, there was little demand for their work.

Before applying for government assistance, however, Barlow worked as a jewelry designer, determined to earn enough money to finance a trip to Europe. Having saved $500, and armed with letters of introduction from the president of the National Academy, he and Ilya Bolotowsky, the precisionist painter, bicycled through Europe during 1931 visiting major museums and important private collections. Returning to New York in 1932, Barlow joined the 3,749 artists who, nationally, produced more than 15,633 works of art before the Public Works of Art Project was liquidated in 1934. Establishment of the Federal Art Project not only provided continuing employment by the government, but also became the major reason for his development as a skilled printmaker whose primary mode of expression was wood engraving.

During a recent telephone conversation with Mr. Barlow, he verified that the *Tenant Farmers* in this exhibition is one of the five complementary prints given to the artist by the workshop supervisor at the time the edition of 25 was printed. In his private collection until 1980, this print was signed that year when it was sold as a result of a one man exhibition held during that year. The print, done in 1936, was therefore not signed by the artist until 1980. The approximate date of 1939 was apparently established by a subsequent seller who was aware of its Project origins. The obligatory 25 prints of this image for allocation to tax supported institutions would have the signature "Louis Breslow," a name the artist changed in 1951 to Lou Barlow. Inasmuch as the print in this exhibition is signed "Lou Barlow," the artist has confirmed it is originally from his own collection.

Tenant Farmers is a compelling image of a weary rural couple whose despair and dejection is apparent in the lined, humorless faces and the dark shadows around the eyes of both people. Barlow has eloquently expressed the effect of the harsh climate of the depression, literally and emotionally, with angular precise representation of people and their demanding existence.

Barlow terminated his association with the graphic arts division in 1941 after which he served as a medical illustrator with the army during the second World War. Work he did in this capacity was routinely sent to Washington where it was published in medical bulletins. After his discharge from the army, he continued in medical illustration, to which he added the unique skill of creating prosthetics from 1942 until 1980, accumulating a total of 44 years as a medical artist. Since retirement he has resumed printmaking, but has discovered that end grain blocks for wood engraving are in extremely short supply and is, therefore, concentrating on linoleum cut instead.

Tenant Farmers, 1936
Colored Wood Engraving
7⅞ x 10⅞ in.
Stamped New York City
WPA Art Project

Reference:
Personal interview with arti
January 22, 1988.

THOMAS HART BENTON

DURING THE 1930's, the mid section of the United States, the sizable middle west, was the geographic, and thus the economic and cultural, crossroads between the industrial east and the still remote west. There was, among some American intellectuals, a sense of disillusionment about what they perceived as a naive, provincial, inadequate American culture which could not hope to compare favorably with European intellectual tradition. Thomas Hart Benton, however, did not see a culturally barren America, and was determined to emphasize the excitement of those national qualities which were unique to the democratic ideals on which the country had been founded. Benton saw his art as an aesthetic symbol of the ongoing search for a national identity, and a revival of nationalist political attitudes which had surfaced after President Wilson and his internationalist policies were defeated.

Many of Benton's prints, like those of John Steuart Curry and Grant Wood, were self-conscious re-statements of themes first explored in his paintings. *Cradling Wheat*, 1939, for example, is after a painting, 30″ x 40″, with the same title, done in 1938 and which is in the City Art Museum of St. Louis, St. Louis, Missouri. The subject is a scene in rural East Tennessee observed by Benton in 1928. Benton began working in lithography in 1929 and, although he liked the tonal range possible with the process, he could claim no technical innovations with it.[1] He had met George Miller, the master lithographic printer, and collaborated closely with him, with Miller printing all the lithographs he produced through 1935. In July 1934, Benton became associated with Reeves Lewenthal who proposed a plan by which prints could be marketed by mail order and in department stores across the country.[2] Named the Association of American Artists, it became an art gallery operation which offered artists the attractive possibility of printing editions of 250, allowing sale prices of as low as five dollars for some prints. Artists were to be paid a flat fee of two hundred dollars per image, with bonuses when images from ten stones or plates were sold out.

The relationship between printmakers and the Associated American Artists group was mutually beneficial. In Benton's case specifically, the AAA circulated fifty of his eighty lithographs, and sold about 12,000 individual prints.[3] Lewenthal's merchandising ideas were certainly progressive, and succeeded in modifying the concept of art as a luxury available only in galleries catering to those who could afford high prices. Art, in this way, became a popular product, widely available to Americans who bought more original works by living American artists than ever before in history.

Cradling Wheat, 1939
Lithograph
12 x 9¾ in.
Edition 250
Circulated by Associated American Artists, New York City

[1] Creekmore Fath, ed., *The Lithographs of Thomas Hart Benton* (Austin: The University of Texas, 1969), p. 15.
[2] Fath, p. 17.
[3] Fath, p. 18.

HENRY BILLINGS

MACHINES AND MACHINERY became increasingly important sources of imagery for artists as the depression of the 1930's worsened and the numbers of jobless increased. Inevitably many unemployed skilled workers were convinced they had been displaced by machines which could work faster and more efficiently than people. Other opinions, however, included a realization that mechanization had the potential of improving the economy and raising the standard of living. Furthermore, it was reassuring for many to note that machinery required the control of skilled operators who could competently use machines as extensions of a human intellect.

Although some people were, indeed, displaced from their jobs by machines, many recognized that the eventual streamlining of the work force would be a beneficial outcome. This attitude was evident in all countries affected by the depression. For example, a widely read French work, *Le grand releve des hommes par la machine*, by Jacques Duboin, proposed that workers were being replaced by machines because "mechanization makes possible the multiplication of output without any increase in labor."[1] It further declared that unemployment was an advantage for humanity, not a disadvantage, because it allowed everyone to work shorter hours, then retire when in their fifties. In the United States, Lewis Mumford authored a work titled *Technics and Civilization*, published in 1934, which argued that technological unemployment was a liberating, not an oppressive, factor in human life.[2] The need for exerting rational control over economic activity was becoming obvious, and careful planning of production and distribution methods became a necessity.

In the lithograph reproduced here, Henry Billings has created a visual interpretation of that point of view. Man and machine are interdependent, and combine to form a unique and efficient partnership. For the printmaker to whom precision and craftsmanship are essential, a close examination of a machinist's method of determining precise measurements is a logical choice for a design. Billings once said: "Machines have become America's mythology. They are our saints, our Pan, our Muses. The traditional symbols are dead, and have no place in the actualities of American life."[3] If machines had become the most relevant cultural symbols, the graphic artist of the thirties became the worker who interpreted and conventionalized those symbols. With a level of skill equal to that of the machinist depicted here, Billings places the viewer in the work in order to complete the composition. Billings' clean, crisp style helps convey a sense of organization, precision and an almost sanitary environment. His workers do not exist in a disorderly factory or a cluttered construction site, they seem to inhabit laboratory-like settings where even the metal shavings arrange themselves in tidy patterns and spirals. Perhaps the machine was viewed as the industrial saviour which would finally order the social and economic chaos of the time.

Men and Machines, 1931
Lithograph
14 x 16 in.

[1] John A. Garraty, *The Great Depression* (Garden City, New York: 1987), p. 136.
[2] Garraty, p. 137.
[3] *Arts International.* Volume 2 (1980), p. 46.

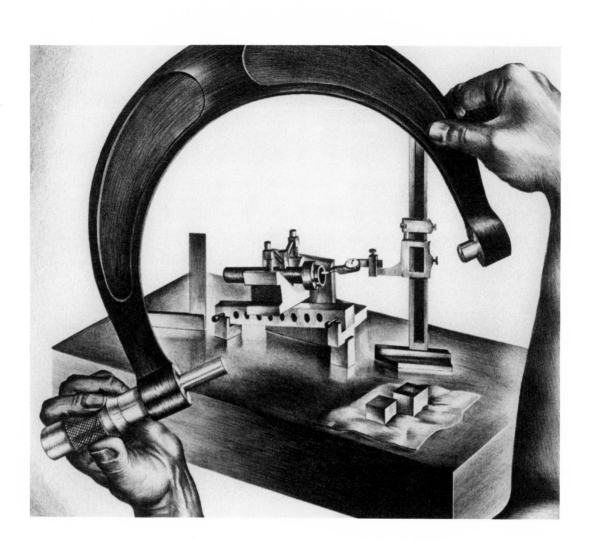

PRINTMAKING FIRST ATTRACTED John Steuart Curry's attention in 1927 while he was studying at the Art Student's League in New York, and continued to interest him until near the end of his career.[1] Curry's lithographs often derived from his paintings, but just as frequently they were sources for paintings. *Prize Stallions,* reproduced at the right, originated as *Belgian Stallions* (1938), an oil painting. It represents a man leading an enormous stallion, startled and aggressive, through a narrow runway into the arena of the University Stock Pavilion at the University of Wisconsin.[2] The Belgian, the most popular draft horse breed in the United States during the thirties, was favored by American farmers because of its docile, easy-going temperament.[3] The horse represented here, however, hardly seems docile. Curry has caught it in a moment of indecision, hesitating in its step forward as, with head thrown back and nostrils flaring, it is confronted by the sight and noise of the crowd inside the pavilion.

While Reginald Marsh, an urban artist also represented in this exhibition, portrayed a wooden carousel horse, Curry, the regionalist, depicted a vigorous, living animal. And yet, it is a horse bred for hard work and pulling heavy loads, whose days of usefulness are numbered as those of its urban cousin had been only a few decades earlier. The number of registered draft animals in the United States declined from approximately 95,000 in 1920 to only a few thousand by 1945.[4] The depressed economic conditions of the thirties forced many small farmers and tenant farmers from their land, and mechanization replaced the horse as a means of lowering production costs on larger farms.[5] And so, the proud animal here, while not destined for a dog food factory like many of its lesser bred brothers, nevertheless represents a dying breed. It shakes its head defiantly and pulls away from the farmer it has served, as if unwilling to relinquish its important place on the American farm. Curry has captured a slice of American history that passed with the coming of the greater horse-power of machines.

Like Grant Wood and Thomas Hart Benton, Curry's lithographs were marketed by Reeves Lewenthal of the Associated American Artists in major department stores throughout the country. Lewenthal was convinced that prints produced in large editions of 250 impressions could be priced at an affordable five dollars each, guaranteeing sales. Prints by some artists, including Curry, sold out quickly, while others were slow moving.[6] This popularity was partially due to Curry's rural regionalist tendencies toward nostalgic images, often visual verifications of past memories with which most viewers can identify. But Curry's work was more than merely simple depictions of the agricultural mid-west; he also portrayed the often brutal battles with wind, floods, and tornadoes which were part of an existence which was not always idyllic.

Prize Stallions, 1938
Lithograph
12¾ x 8¾ in.
Edition: 250
Associated American Artis

[1] *Lithographs of John Steuart Curry,* comp. and ed. Sylva Cole, Jr. (New York: Ameri Artists, 1976), from intro b Laurence E. Schmeckebier, ┇

[2] Laurence E. Schmeckebier, *John Steuart Curry's Pageant America.* (New York: Ameri Artist's Group, 1943), p. 19

[3] L. Dale Van Vleck, "Breeds the United States," from *Th Horse,* eds. J. Warren Evans al. (San Francisco: W.H. Freeman and Co., 1977), p.

[4] Van Vleck, p. 193.

[5] Francis Haines, *Horses in America.* (New York: Thom Y. Crowell Co., 1971), p. 19

[6] Clinton Adams, *American Lithographers 1900–1960* (Albuquerque: University o New Mexico Press, 1983), p. 1

33

ISAC FRIEDLANDER

STRONG DESIGN CHARACTERIZES the work of Isac Friedlander, represented here with *Warming Up,* ca. 1935. Like many of his colleagues also assigned to the graphic arts division of the Federal Art Project, Friedlander was a champion of the downtrodden and the outcast. In too many cases the outcast were recently unemployed workers overwhelmed by the magnitude of the nationwide economic crisis and, therefore, uncertain of their immediate prospects. These were not the slothful, nor were they out of work either by choice or because of poor performance on the job. These unemployed had lost control of their own destinies causing a predictable emotional apathy which accounted for large numbers of derelicts, or "bums," on the streets. Social and economic mobility was severely curtailed, the unemployed could not afford to look for work outside their immediate communities, nor were they financially able to re-locate even if they could secure employment elsewhere. Not surprisingly, the general climate was one of pessimism and lethargy.

Warming Up poses numerous questions, but suggests few answers. Norman Barr, President of the New York Artists, Inc. observed that: "To understand fully the meaning of the Great Depression, one must go beyond the statistics, as staggering as they are to a rational mind."[1] He recalled shanties built of cardboard, tin, wooden planks and whatever else could be found which housed people along the Hudson, Harlem and East Rivers in New York. These deplorable and inadequate shelters which housed a majority of the starving, destitute population of the city were called "Hoovervilles" and were a major factor in identifying catastrophic effects of the depression in terms of human dignity.

Artists, such as Friedlander, were equally desperate, but had a psychological advantage in that they were determined to continue working as artists in spite of enormous obstacles. It seemed to be this growing sense of artistic identity that provided artists with a purpose that was to see them acquire, finally, recognition as hard-working, skilled members of society. Their tenacity and dedication forestalled the despair experienced by laborers who became convinced of their worthlessness and were increasingly unable to find work. Artists, on the other hand, became more sure of themselves as they gained public recognition and support by government agencies, and as they developed an important sense of a working community. Those who survive today still speak of a warm feeling evoked by memories of their experiences on the Federal Art Project, a glow which Emily Grenauer suggests may recall a time when artists stood together to keep warm around a government-lighted bonfire.[2]

Warming Up, ca. 1935
Etching
9¾ x 11⅞ in.

[1] Norman Barr, "Statement," *New York City WPA Art, T* 1934–1943 and Now 1960–N Exhibition Catalog (New York: New York City WPA Artists, Inc., 1977), p. xiv.

[2] Emily Grenauer, "WPA Influences," *New York City WPA Art, Then 1934–1943* *Now 1960–1977* Exhibition Catalog (New York: New Y City WPA Artists, Inc., 198 p. vii.

LEON GILMOUR

THE APPARENTLY ANONYMOUS American worker of the depression, as interpreted by Leon Gilmour, is the predictable image of physical strength associated with much of the art produced under the auspices of the Federal Art Project. Strong men engaged in strenuous, productive activity during the years of unemployment are usually seen as portrayals of optimism for the benefit of the viewing public at large for whom government sponsored art was intended. As early as 1933 the short lived Public Works of Art Project provided support for artists, regardless of ability, who were unemployed, thereby establishing at the outset a direct association of artist with worker. Gilmour's print reflects the sympathetic ideal of the laborer who symbolized the trust in a better tomorrow which was so necessary to American morale during the thirties.

Leon Gilmour was nine years old when he arrived in this country in 1916, one of nearly nine million immigrants processed through Ellis Island during the earliest years of the 20th century. Although determined to become an artist, he could not afford to complete his education and was forced to seek employment as a construction worker in New York, then as a field hand in the mid-west, a gold miner in Colorado and, finally, a truck driver in Los Angeles.[1] Gilmour's ability to portray the essential qualities which characterize the typical American worker must be seen as a result of the diversity of those experiences.

In *Cement Finishers* (1939), reproduced here, two men are finishing the cement around a large pipe. One man, his back to the viewer, seems distracted, while the second attends to his task. The crane in the background serves both as a visual comment on the inevitable and increasing reliance on the machine, and as a compositional device which unifies men and machine by organizing the major elements into a stable triangular shape. Instead of resisting modern mechanization, these workers are in harmony with it.

The figure leaning forward, a black man, is an element which serves as a reminder of the consciousness on the part of the Federal Art Project of its role in the need to improve race relations. In general, there was little discrimination on the part of project administrators, and black artists were accorded opportunities equal to everyone else. In July, 1937, the New York City project listed 115 black artists, including three supervisors.[2] While the Federal Art Project definitely afforded new opportunities for black artists, and for art education in black communities, blacks in turn made significant contributions.[3]

Cement Finishers, 1939
Wood Engraving
10⅛ x 8⅛ in.

[1] "Leon Gilmour: Wood Engra Printmaker," Associated American Artists.
[2] William F. McDonald, *Fede Relief Administration and the Arts.* (Ohio: Ohio State University Press, 1969), p.
[3] McDonald, p. 414.

AWARDED A GUGGENHEIM FELLOWSHIP to study in Europe for a year, Harry Gottlieb returned to New York City in 1934 to find his country in crisis. To Gottlieb, however, the thirties became a time of integration for him, both as artist and citizen. He could, and did, align himself with causes and organizations whose goals included recognition of the professional respect artists deserved and their acceptance into communities of like-minded workers. The social environment of the depression increased Gottlieb's awareness of the potential of what he discerned as new subject matter, which included people who were out of work and destitute, as well as the drama and excitement of the more fortunate who were working, especially those working with steel construction.

Gottlieb worked with the silk screen unit of the graphic arts workshop in New York, and gives Anthony Velonis credit for establishing this aspect of the Project.[1] Velonis also taught the process to artists eager to learn this technique which, although not new, was so clearly a method of producing prints in the numbers requested by the Federal Art Project. According to Gottlieb: "American people cannot afford oil paintings, or even watercolors, yet they want pictures in their homes. The sharecropper tacks up pictures from the Sunday paper; screen prints can provide an art which people can afford to buy." Equipment for screen printing was simple, light, inexpensive, and, according to Gottlieb, allowed an artist to turn out editions of as many as 1,000. When Gottlieb listed the prints he had produced as a project artist, he also included the number of colors in each print, which ranged from three to eleven.

An activist in organizations dedicated to increasing public awareness of problems unique to artists, Gottlieb, along with Chet LaMore and Louis Lozowick, spoke on "Freedom of Expression in Art" at the first meeting of the Congress of American Artists on June 6, 1936. He was also among those who signed the Call to a Congress of American Artists in 1941 to address concerns specific to artists, including developing new audiences for art and promoting a cultural exchange between peoples of the Americas. Gottlieb, who is still working in his New York studio, repeated during a recent conversation his conviction that artists during the thirties had to be politically active if they expected to move ahead. In order to do so, he said, artists had to be in agreement on principles important to their purposes.[2]

Change of Shift, 1940, is an example of Gottlieb's strong, direct style which depends on large areas of flat color, and which was so naturally adapted to screen printing. It effectively illustrates his stated goal of attempting an honest communication, in aesthetic terms, of the essence of the worker experience. Gottlieb's workers are energetic, enthusiastic and ambitious. They are no longer the despondent, languishing figures often seen in prints of the earlier depression, but demonstrate the sense of an optimistic future which busy factories promised.

Change of Shift, 1940
Serigraph, WPA stamp
16 ¾ x 20 in.

[1] Archives of American Art The Gottlieb Papers, Roll Number D 343.
[2] Personal interview with art January 29, 1988.

IRWIN D. HOFFMAN

SYMPATHETIC RESPONSE TO MINERS, their lives and working conditions, characterizes much of Irwin Hoffman's work. In a genuine attempt to understand the problems miners encounter daily, Hoffman spent considerable time underground observing first hand their working conditions and ways of relaxing. He listened to their discussions about difficulties and disagreements with mine supervisors, and the general need for improved conditions. Hoffman invested the workers he portrayed with a laconic dignity consistent with his sympathetic understanding of the typical demeanor of men whose working lives are spent in hazardous occupations.

Cigarette Underground, ca. 1938, is a study of a miner taking a necessary short break, probably one of many during the course of a working day, from the arduous labor of cutting through solid underground rock. These short breaks typically lasted for about five minutes, the time needed to smoke a cigarette and relax as totally as possible. This and similar studies were done in the Moranda gold and copper mine in Quebec, a non-ferrous mine where cigarette smoking was not the perilous activity it would have been in a coal mine.[1] However, soft rock and carbide lamps contributed a definite element of risk. Hoffman's portrayals of these humble, hard-working men are neither sentimental nor sociological, simply straightforward observations of the human spirit under relentless tension. The miner in this print is lighting his cigarette with a flare lamp that illuminates his "grimy, sooty furrowed face, he holds the lamp with hands so dirty, roughened and calloused by years of labor, they no longer come clean."[2]

Hoffman, born in 1901 in Boston, studied art at the School of Fine Arts of the Boston Museum. He was awarded the Page Travelling Scholarship in 1924, allowing him to continue his studies in Paris, Rome, Vienna and Madrid. He spent nearly the entire year of 1929 in Russia, sketching and painting a suffering humanity, a theme which continued to furnish material for his work when he returned home. Brother of two mining engineers, Hoffman had access to mining camps in the western United States and Canada where he again found the simple, unaffected people with whom he felt a kinship as a worker. Assigned only briefly, from March until July 1936, to the Federal Art Project, he travelled and worked in Mexico where he was drawn again to the worker who is reliant on the soil and whose life is continual struggle.[3] Unlike the prevalent theme of oppression and exploitation of the peasant as defined by Diego Rivera and Jose Orozco, Hoffman was interested in the symbiotic relationship between the laborer and his environment.

Cigarette Underground, ca. 1938
Etching
10¾ x 8¹⁵/₁₆ in.
Signed in pencil
Pennell Fund

[1] Albert Reese, *American Pri* *Prints of the 20th Century* (N York: American Artists Gr 1949), p. 87.
[2] *Art Digest*, 12, No. 4 (1937),
[3] *Published Plates of Irwin D. Hoffman* (New York: Associated American Artis 1936). Introduction by Margaret Sullivan.

THE AMERICAN LABOR MOVEMENT and labor conditions of the 1930's were important aspects of society during the depression, and therefore became major elements in art of the period. Directly due to prevailing economic conditions, unemployment and non-regulated labor practices, unions widened their scope and influence, including organizing artists. Many previously non-unionized occupations and professions affiliated with the American Federation of Labor (AFL) or the Congress of Industrial Organizations (CIO). Having developed an awareness of their association with workers in American society, artists organized in 1934 into the Artists Union, a trade organization.[1] Joe Jones, born Joseph John Jones in 1909 in St. Louis, Missouri, whose work is reproduced here, was an advocate of the Artists Union as well as those responsible for having organized it, the Unemployed Artists Group.[2] Jones was not only an active participant in organizing artists into militant unions, but was known for sympathetic depictions of American workers in his art. He received early recognition for his work, including the Guggenheim Fellowship, awarded him in 1937. His work is represented in collections of the Whitney Museum of American Art, the Metropolitan Museum of Art and the Library of Congress. Primarily a painter, Jones also worked as a draftsman and graphic artist. In addition, he painted murals, under sponsorship of the Federal Art Project, for post offices in Anthony, Kansas in 1939 and Seneca, Kansas in 1940, but had a design rejected by the jury for the St. Louis competition, presumably because the style was not conservative enough for the community.[3]

The untitled lithograph reproduced here, referred to as *Harvest Workers* (ca. 1940), appears to contradict his murals in which the harvesting of crops is performed by machines, not by men.[4] It does, however, present a realistic view of prevailing conditions in harvest camps of the time during which these itinerant workers were not organized and working conditions were neither regulated nor humane. Like tenant farmers, these migrants were the first to be displaced when farmers suffered reversals or lost their lands. An active member of the Artists Union, Jones believed firmly in the power of organized labor, and was acutely sensitive to the appallingly adverse conditions which farm workers were often compelled to endure. In a July, 1935 issue of *The Art Front*, Clarence Weinstock wrote that Jones saw himself as "subject to society, bounded by enmities and alliances, member of a class: a worker." This close identification with workers is apparent in the agitated linear organization of two forlorn laborers huddled together to make a militantly expressive comment.

Untitled *(Harvest Worker*
ca. 1940
Lithograph
9⅞ x 8 in.

[1] Gerald M. Monroe, "Artis Militant Trade Union Wo During the Great Depress *Archives of American Art Jo*ı 14, No. 1 (1974).
[2] Monroe, "Art Front," *Arch of American Art Journal*, 1. No. 3 (1973).
[3] Karal Ann Marling, *Wall-Wall America*. (Minneapol University of Minnesota Press, 1982), p. 295.
[4] Marling, pp. 122, 295.

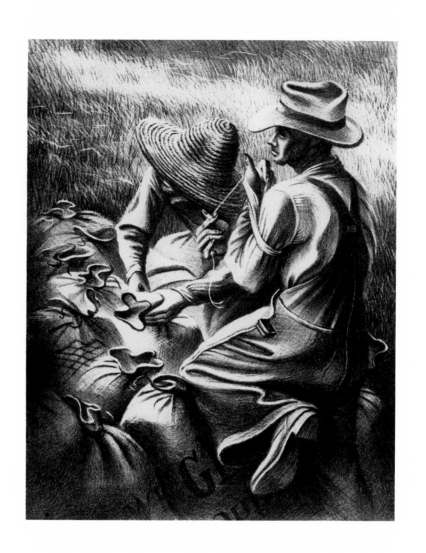

CHET LA MORE

BORN IN DANE CITY, Wisconsin on July 30, 1908, Chet LaMore earned the B.A. and M.A. degrees from the University of Wisconsin after which he taught art, history of art and art criticism at the University of Wisconsin, Ohio State University and the Albright Art School in Buffalo, New York. In 1936 he did further graduate work in Art Education at Columbia University, and worked for the WPA/FAP from May 16, 1937 until August 24, 1939. In 1937 he was elected chairman of the Artist's Union which had been organized for the specific purpose of securing and insuring work relief for artists. The Artist's Union published The Art Front, of which both Ben Shahn and Stuart Davis were editors, and to which some of the more radical artists, including Louis Lozowick and William Gropper, contributed. LaMore was a militant advocate of the rights of artists during the depression, fighting aggressively to keep artists from the ever present danger of being cut from WPA rolls.[1] For example, when printmakers submitted proposals to the supervisor of the graphic arts division to be considered by the "subjects and approvals committee," there were two persons present to represent project workers who were selected from a list submitted by the Artist's Union. Although these two representatives had no vote, they could, and often did, protest rejections they considered to be inequitable.

LaMore acknowledged repeatedly the sense of artistic community which dominated the years 1936–1939. The FAP, he said, enabled him to live and work in New York at a time when he most needed contact with other artists, and the invaluable resources provided by museums all of which were in close proximity.[2] He noted that this was a unique period in the history of American art in that, in spite of the usual contentions between abstractionists and realists, the old guard and young innovators, all artists worked together in a non-competitive environment. As diverse and individual as they were, these artists nevertheless isolated themselves from "dealers, patrons, decorators, promoters and art critics."[3] LaMore found the FAP so open minded and democratic that it was almost too permissive, an error he acknowledged to be preferable to the alternative of inflexibility.

Working in both lithography and wood engraving, LaMore created unusually strong and straightforward representations of workers in industry and mining. In the untitled lithograph of automobile workers done in 1937, there is a selected detail of a production line which seems more leisurely than busy. This may be one of the final stages during which the automobiles are primed and painted. The artist's pride in the technicalities of his craft may be portrayed in the central figure's careful concentration on his task. In contrast to today's worker who would demonstrate concern for his own safety by wearing mask and goggles, the worker of the 1930's, unaware of potential hazards, focused his undivided attention on the all important job.

Untitled (Auto Worker),
1937
12 x 14⅞ in.
WPA Lithograph

[1] Chet LaMore, Archives of American Art, Roll D 343.
[2] Archives, Roll D 343.
[3] Francis V. O'Connor, *Federal Support for the Visual Arts: The New Deal Then and Now* (Greenwich, CT: New York Graphic Society, Ltd., 1969) p. 96.

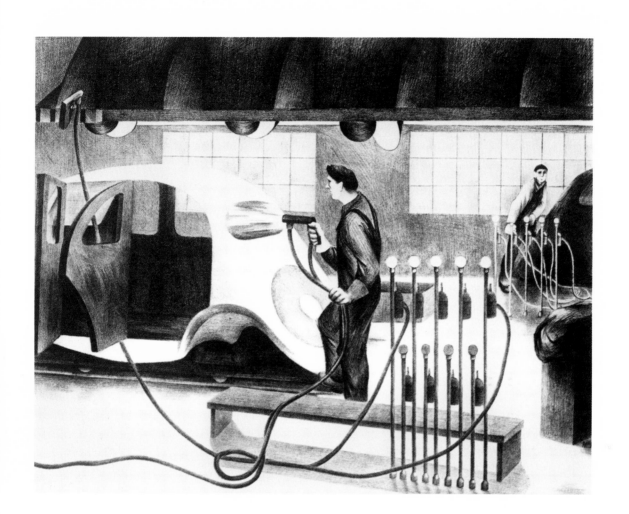

PAUL LANDACRE

WOOD ENGRAVING, one of the major printmaking processes supported by the FAP, has virtually disappeared as a mode of artistic expression. Admittedly tedious and slow, wood engraving nevertheless offers subtle linear effects not easily obtained with other methods. Paul Landacre experimented with various graphic techniques before settling on wood engraving. He devoted years to perfecting his engraving and printing techniques, then developing his creative abilities. He did his own printing and continuously tried different combinations of papers and inks.[1] Critical evaluations of his work usually include mention of the high degree of technical skill evident in his prints. The printmaker is craftsman as well as creative artist, and Landacre noted the importance of the process, which is perhaps more workmanlike in printing than in the other fine arts, when he said, "there is the physical pleasure of the feel of the graver in boxwood, and the fascinating and exasperating mechanics of printing, and . . . the marvellous feeling of having completed something."[2] Landacre won numerous awards for his prints, and his work is represented in the collections of the New York Public Library, the Boston Museum of Fine Art, the San Francisco Museum of Fine Art, the Library of Congress, and the Museum of Modern Art.

Landacre was born into a family of scientists and teachers in Columbus, Ohio, and apparently intended to continue in that tradition when he studied entomology at Ohio State. However, a streptococcus infection in 1922 left him crippled and forced him to move to California.[3] He married Margaret McCreery in 1925, and with her encouragement and support, concentrated on developing his printmaking abilities.

This exhibition includes two somewhat enigmatic works by Landacre, *Poachers* (1934) and *Amateurs* (1937). In *Amateurs*, reproduced here, three men are involved in roofing a building, but only one of the men is actually working. The second rubs his shoulder, perhaps unaccustomed to physical labor, while tar drips from his brush onto the roof. The third stares vacantly into space, either unaware of, or indifferent to, the spilled can of tar creating a mess at his feet. Threatening clouds and wind-bent trees indicate an approaching storm, a fact that should but does not lend any feeling of urgency to their task.

The print may be a humorous portrayal of several unskilled laborers, not properly trained for their work, and may have resulted from Landacre's own experiences building an addition onto his house during 1937, the year this print is dated. It may simply be a statement about untidy and careless work by a man who was in his own work technically superb, and valued fine craftsmanship. But it may also be a much more serious look at the malaise of workers disheartened and dispirited by the continued severity of the depression. As a wood engraver he identified with skilled laborers who worked with their hands, was particularly aware of the satisfaction found in fine craftsmanship, and acutely sensitive to the shoddy workmanship portrayed in this print. The strong vertical and diagonal lines in the work produce a sense of tension in direct contrast to the careless attitudes displayed by the workers. The threatening black clouds augment this tension, to produce a critical statement aimed less at the careless workers than at the system which has allowed them to lose a sense of purpose.

Amateurs, 1937
Wood Engraving
7 x 11 in.

[1] Margaret McCreery, "The Woodcut Prints of Paul Landacre." *The Print Connoisseur* (1932): p. 124.
[2] Carl Zigrosser, "Paul Landacre," *The Artist in America: Twentyfour Close-Ups of Contemporary Printmakers.* (New York: Alfred A. Knopf, 1942), p. 155.
[3] Zigrosser, p. 153.

CLARE LEIGHTON

THE ONLY WOMAN ARTIST included in this exhibition, Clare Leighton was born in London in 1901, and educated at the Brighton School of Art and the Slade School of Fine Arts. She made her first wood engraving in 1923, and soon achieved recognition as an illustrator. She lectured in the United States in 1925 and 1926, settled permanently in New England in 1939, and still lives in her Connecticut home. She has illustrated several books, including Thomas Hardy's *Return of the Native* and Emily Bronte's *Wuthering Heights,* and has also written and illustrated fourteen of her own books,[1] the most famous being *The Farmer's Year,* a seasonal exploration of British agricultural life. Four prints from *The Farmer's Year* and two from her Lumber Camp series, made during a two month stay at a Canadian lumber camp, are included in this exhibition. She has received numerous honors, and her work is found in the collections of the Metropolitan Museum of Art, the New York Public Library, the Library of Congress, the British Museum, and the Victoria and Albert Museum.

Although Leighton did not become a naturalized citizen until 1945, and never worked for the FAP, her philosophies about printmaking were shared by many American artists working during the depression. She believes in art for the people, not just for an elite few, and her identification of the scientific spirit of observation as an aspect of printmaking[2] links her with artists such as Henry Billings. However, she also relates directly to them in her perceptions of artist as worker. In *The Farmer's Year,* she described the farmer planning his activity for the year:

> The farmer sits throughout the long evenings in the farm kitchen, slowly and with many falterings making out his plans for the year. . . . The oil-lamp. . .throws a circle of light upon him and his note-book and stump of pencil that are to determine by a few scribbles on paper the face of the land through the year. By this stump of pencil is decided the fate of this calf and that sow. . . .So is the pattern of the year designed out of the farmer's brain.[3]

Leighton's description of the farmer's evening work sounds uncannily like her later description of her own work as an artist, planning the design of a wood engraving:

> I would do a few rough lines of ideas for designs. When I start a design, the minimum of lines suffices to secure the pattern and the essential rhythm. . . . I develop it then, further and further. . . . It is a wonderful moment, for the scribbled lines seem to happen beyond all conscious control. . .later. . .the artist is faced with the struggle to keep the spirit of his work alive throughout the tedium of execution.[4]

Both descriptions share the same "scribbled lines on paper," planning in one case the landscape of the farmer's year, and in the other, the landscape of the engraving. Both farmer and artist must then spend long hours at their work to bring their plans to fruition. It is this sort of identification of artist with worker that links Leighton's work to many of the prints produced during the depression.

Plowing, 1932
Wood Engraving
7⅞ x 10¼ in.

[1] "Clare Leighton Wood Engravings," exhibition pamph[l] Associated American Artis[ts] (New York: Associated American Artists, 1983), unpaginated.

[2] Sybil Vincent, "In the Stud[io] of Clare Leighton," *London Studio* 13 (Jan. – June 1937): p. 146.

[3] Clare Leighton, *The Farmer['s] Year.* (New York: Longmans, Green and Co., 1933), p. 10[.]

[4] Clare Leighton, "How I Ma[de] My Book," *American Artist* [19] (Feb. 1955): pp. 41, 43.

HERSCHEL LEVIT

ALTHOUGH HERSCHEL LEVIT is now an art historian, much of his early career was devoted to the production of visual art. Born in Pennsylvania in 1912, he was a young, practicing printmaker during the depression, but apparently abandoned that work 30 years ago in favor of teaching the history of art and architecture. Author of *French Gothic Art and Architecture* and *Views of Rome—Then and Now,* his interest in architectural structures has spanned many different times and places.[1] However, as a young man living and working in the United States during the depression, he naturally turned his attention toward the more immediate and accessible architectonic forms around him. The logical subjects for his work were the massive construction projects of that period. Although there is a tendency to think of the depression as a period of nearly complete economic inactivity, significant projects were being funded by Congress for the WPA and the Bureau of Reclamation among other government agencies. These government sponsored projects played an essential role in shoring up the American economy in the attempt to maintain a semblance of economic normalcy.[2]

Levit forcefully and accurately illustrated workers on these construction projects. *Dam Builders* (1937) depicts construction of an anonymous dam somewhere in the United States. The powerful diagonal lines of the cranes and cables repeat and emphasize the muscular figures of the men working with them. The more conservative horizontal lines, which represent the infrastructure of the cement dam, provide a background for the foreground activity. Neither too strong nor too weak, the horizontal elements are an effective foil for the powerful figures of the men. This forcefulness is accentuated by the superhuman, almost heroic, proportions of the dam builders. Even the unnatural foreshortening of the arms of these workers only adds to the feeling of great strength. Their muscular arms, necks and backs confirm the extent of the physical exertion demanded during construction of such a monumental project. Placement of the figures close to the frontal plane is a compositional device which reinforces the concept that the working man is capable of dominating and controlling natural forces. Does it also imply that the working class can exert control over man-made political and economic forces?

Like the Federal Art Project, government sponsored construction programs were designed to remove the unemployed from relief rolls, and were intended to improve living and working conditions.[3] Intentionally or not, these projects also provided men and women assigned to them a feeling of achievement without the loss of human dignity often suffered by welfare recipients who did not work. It was this sense of worthwhile endeavor which also encouraged artists by acknowledgement that their work was as legitimate as that performed by construction and industrial laborers. Workers, including artists, assumed an unprecedented position in society, a fact which accounted for a proclivity on the part of artists to render impressions of Americans at work. Levit the worker depicts here the importance of labor in contemporary society; Levit the artist is contributing an important ingredient to the development of a unique American style.

Dam Builders, 1937
Lithograph
9¼ x 12¼ in.

LOUIS LOZOWICK

SLEEK TOWERS and stepped ziggurat-like forms identify the New York skyline in Louis Lozowick's powerful *Through Brooklyn Bridge Cables* (1938), a lithograph completed during the period between 1935 and 1940 when the artist worked on the Graphic Arts Division of the Federal Art Project. Born in the Kiev district of Russia in 1892, Lozowick arrived in the United States in 1906, already trained in traditional methods, and having absorbed the philosophy that "the artist is one with a noble mission."[1] Although he continued his study of art in this country, Lozowick felt a strong need to return to Europe in 1920 for further exposure to the concepts of order and discipline which formed the philosophical foundations of Constructivism, Purism, DeStijl and the Bauhaus. Systematic order was considered essential for relevant artistic reactions to mechanization and industrialism which were rapidly dominating urban society throughout the world. Lozowick, like many other artists of his time, believed the machine was a positive force and that visual representations of machinery should emphasize their potential as tools for effecting democratic progress.

While in Berlin in 1923, Lozowick was introduced to lithography, the revival of which had swept through Europe by then. The explorative directions in graphic arts to which he was exposed encouraged him to continue working in printmaking upon his return to the United States. Carl Zigrosser of the Weyhe Gallery supported Lozowick's interest in this process by giving him a one man exhibition of recent lithographs in 1929. In 1931 he was awarded the Cleveland Print Club's $1,000 first prize, and in 1931 he received the Mary S. Collins Prize for best lithograph in the Third Exhibition of the Philadelphia Print Club. In her Catalog Raisonne, Janet Flint observed that Lozowick had an instinctive affinity for the medium which was apparent from the beginning, and continued to develop a personal repertoire of techniques over the years.[2]

Having assimilated constructivist and cubist theories in Europe, Lozowick was prepared to meet the challenge presented by a rapidly growing city by creating views of New York skyscrapers as modern symbols of optimism. Lozowick, like other artists during the depression, identified closely with the worker of his time, invariably thinking of his own involvement with the printmaking process and its products in terms of craft and workmanship.[3]

Assigned to the New York Graphic Arts Division in 1935, Lozowick left to accept a major commission from the more prestigious Treasury Relief Art Project for two large oil paintings for the post office at 33rd Street, Manhattan, which occupied his time completely during 1936–1937.

Characteristically, his preliminary studies for the paintings were lithographs which are among his strongest images of New York skyscraper and bridge forms made comprehensible by the artist's imposition of a rational structure. Returning to the Project in 1938, Lozowick concentrated on experimental printmaking, including wood engraving, drypoint and screen printing, until his appointment was terminated in 1940 after which he devoted himself exclusively to lithography.

Through Brooklyn Bridge Cables, 1938
Lithograph
9⅝ x 12¹³⁄₁₆ in.
Edition: 15; printed in 1939 for Associated American Artists in an edition of 250; printed by George C. Miller, ACH

[1] Janet Flint, *The Prints of Louis Lozowick*, Hudson Hills Press, New York, 1982, p. 13. Flint's work offers the most comprehensive treatment of Lozowick and his work to date.
[2] Flint, p. 21.
[3] Flint, p. 26.

SAMUEL L. MARGOLIES

NEW YORK CITY under continuing construction is the theme of this etching, *Builders of Babylon* (1937) by Samuel L. Margolies. During that year the depressed economy had indicated signs of recovery which contributed to a general sense of optimism nationwide, and which is evident in this work.

Two men are riding a steel girder, with the skyline of New York at their feet. These figures, although not heroic in scale, dominate the city which they, and their fellow workers, have created. If the artist's intention is to convey a sense of "urban optimism," defined by art historian Joshua Taylor as "an emotive belief in the promise of tomorrow,"[1] the structure of the city below is an equally important aspect of the composition. Relating workers of the thirties to the optimistic view of a city which is growing creates a view of the depression generally not acknowledged. Construction continued, jobs were available, and not everyone was on relief.

Not only did the role of the laborer in society interest artists, they were also intrigued with the size and scale of the new urban buildings. Margolies ". . .watched the metropolis finger its way skyward. The power and strength of the great city—and the courage of the men who build it—have been poured into his etchings."[2] Born in 1898, Margolies lived and worked in New York during the 1930's. He studied at the National Academy of Design, Cooper Union Art School and the Beaux Arts Institute, acquiring an exceptionally strong exhibition record before he apparently abandoned his professional art career to become a circuit designer in 1939. A member of the American Artists Congress, Margolies exhibited at the New York World's Fair in 1939, and has work in the collections of the Metropolitan Museum of Art, the Library of Congress and various federal buildings in Washington, D.C.[3]

The physical qualities of tall buildings held particular interest for artists working in and around large urban areas during the thirties. Sheer size of skyscrapers caused a profound reaction, and many spoke of these large structures as ageless as the pyramids.[4] That Margolies identified New York with Babylon indicates a belief that the most phenomenal city-state of the ancient Near East had a modern counterpart in the equally phenomenal clustering of monumental skyscrapers within the city.

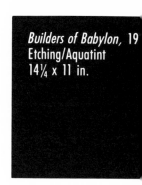

Builders of Babylon, 19
Etching/Aquatint
14¼ x 11 in.

[1] Joshua Taylor, *America As* (1976), p. 192.
[2] Associated American Art artist information, 1940.
[3] Archives of American Ar Artist's Biographical Data Cards, Roll Number 3244 Frame Number 428.
[4] Taylor, p. 194.

ALTHOUGH HE WAS BORN IN PARIS where his American parents were art students, Reginald Marsh was captivated by New York City and the diversity of its people. He first moved to New York as a young man, after graduating from Yale, and worked as a free-lance illustrator for *The Daily News* and *The New Yorker*. He attended classes at the Art Student's League where his instructors included John Sloan and Kenneth Hayes Miller. By the late 1920's, Marsh had virtually abandoned illustration in order to concentrate on painting. The themes which would form the focus of his career emerged quickly: the Bowery, burlesque theaters, the streets of Manhattan and beaches of Coney Island.

Marsh constantly observed the people with whom he shared the city: the unemployed, the derelicts, and especially the women. He shows us burlesque queens, factory workers, shop clerks, secretaries, women at play and strolling during lunch break or dancing with each other in restaurants. The Marsh men typically are indolent, irresolute figures who languish and lounge on street corners or amble aimlessly through railroad yards, all seemingly waiting for the perfect opportunity to present itself. On the other hand, Marsh depicts women as animated, vivacious figures who energetically engage in banal, joyous activities. Large numbers of unemployed men during the depression became "bums" while they waited for job openings consistent with their experience and training. According to one sociological study, work was apparently the sole organizing principle in the lives of middle class American men.[1] An immediate counter effect was an increase of the influence of women whose roles were extended by necessity to include making crucial family decisions and providing emotional support as well as devising endless frugal ways of coping with meager incomes. When women worked outside the home, they willingly accepted any employment, however menial. Unlike men, they did not insist on waiting for jobs for which they were trained; in fact, most had no special skills.

The central figure in *Merry Go Round* (1940), reproduced here, is a self-assured woman, clearly in control of her agitated steed, and who is comfortably integrated within the environment of the carousel. The urban horse of earlier decades has become a lifeless effigy with no purpose except to provide amusement. Characteristically, Marsh introduces sexual tension, but combines it with the tension of a troubled humanity caught in an increasingly mechanized, out-of-control world.[2] The relentless circle of the carousel can be interpreted as symbolic of the feelings experienced by workers during the thirties, caught up in a treadmill with little hope of escape from the dreary realities of life, not even in the fantasy world offered by an amusement park. Marilyn Cohen also describes the dance marathon, a popular event during the thirties, and a theme Marsh often represented, as the "aimless, endless movement of superfluous people around and around. . ."[3] *Merry Go Round* connects the feeling of purposeless movement with a sense of the powerlessness experienced by many unemployed workers, yet it is, simultaneously, an affirmation of the energy and vitality of the human spirit when confronted with an overwhelming situation. Marsh's women never give up, they are self-directed creatures who move forward assertively and assume control of their immediate environment.

Merry Go Round, 1940
Engraving
8 x 12 in.
State I of III

[1] John Garraty, *The Great Depression*. (New York: Harco Brace Jovanovich, 1986), p.
[2] Marilyn Cohen, *Reginald Marsh's New York*. (New Yor Whitney Museum of Ameri Art and Dover Publication 1983), p. 24.
[3] Cohen, p. 6.

ASSIGNED TO THE EASEL DIVISION of the Federal Art Project from 1935 until 1943, Jackson Pollock painted small landscapes which were suitable for allocation to public buildings. Many of these were rural landscapes, ideas for which may have developed from conversations with Thomas Hart Benton, his mentor and friend, who had a summer home on Martha's Vineyard where Pollock was a house guest for several summers. It was during this period that Pollock also produced several lithographs, 12 of which are known to survive. Since he never worked with the graphic division, these were not a part of his Project responsibilities, although he collaborated with Theodore Wahl who printed for artists who were assigned there, and who retained printer's proofs of Pollock's lithographs. These were pulled in small editions, usually only two or three prints, and always in black. Because he was an active member of the Art Student's League from December 1932 until December 1935, Pollock was allowed to use the graphic arts studio on Saturdays where he worked out images for lithographs such as *Stacking Hay*, reproduced at the right. His close association with Benton at the time this print was conceived leads to speculation that the theme may have been inspired by Benton's large commercial editions of popular rural subjects circulated throughout the 1930's by the Associated American Artists.

The linear patterns and organic forms which characterize Benton's work are evident in this print, and may be predictions of Pollock's mature style, variously labeled as "all-over," "gestural" and "action painting." Emphasis on quality of line at the expense of academically correct drawing also suggests an indebtedness to Benton, as does the rural theme, an unusual choice for Pollock. *Stacking Hay* (1936), the Benton-like lithograph reproduced here, was initially titled *The Harvest* and included in a portfolio published in Colorado Springs by Archie Musick.[1]

Although in 1936 he had not yet indicated strong tendencies toward involuntary abstraction, Pollock worked in the experimental mural workshop established by David Alfaro Siqueiros where he observed the then unorthodox use of spray guns, synthetic paints and the "controlled accident."[2] Traditional technique, which was never central to his purpose, must have been more difficult for him after his experience with Siqueiros' strong emphasis on spontaneous application of paint to large surfaces.

Pollock often expressed sincere appreciation for the financial security (wages for the eight years he spent on the Project totalled $7,800) which allowed him to experiment extensively and finally develop the familiar personal style which later defined Abstract Expressionism. Pollock's dependence on the project, which required submission of a painting every eight weeks for allocation, nurtured his developing sense of individual purpose while connecting him directly with the community of artists during the 1930's who were more like laborers than elitist artists who produced images incomprehensible to the majority of the viewing public.

Stacking Hay, c. 1935–
Lithograph
9⅜ x 13 in.
2nd, and final, state
Ed. 60

[1] Clinton Adams, *American Lithographers 1900–1960* (Albuquerque: The Univ of New Mexico Press, 19 p. 127.
[2] Adams, p. 128.

WILLIAM SHARP

AN AUSTRIAN BY BIRTH, William Sharp studied art in Poland, England and France before the first World War. During the war he served in the German army as a machine gunner, then resumed his education at the Art Academies in Munich and Berlin from 1918–1920. As a newspaper illustrator in Berlin during the 1920's, Sharp's political cartoons were comments which strongly opposed the emerging National Socialist movement and, in addition, he regularly submitted drawings to various anti-Nazi publications. Sharp's political views earned him the official disapproval of the government when National Socialism assumed control of Germany in 1933. The threat of imprisonment in a concentration camp brought him to the United States in 1934. In this way, he joined artists such as Hans Hofmann, Josef Albers and Walter Gropius who all left a Germany in which they could no longer work. Hofmann had come from Munich, arriving in New York in 1932, Albers in 1933 and Gropius in 1937.

As an illustrator, Sharp's drawings appeared in the *New York Mirror, Life* magazine, the *New York Times* and *Esquire,* among other newspapers and periodicals. (Among his varied assignments was coverage of the trial of Bruno Richard Hauptman, the accused kidnapper of Charles Lindbergh's infant son.) Naturally interested in current social conditions and their effect on humanity, Sharp chronicled his observations of the depression with a sensitivity which recalls Daumier's anonymous working class people.

Snowflakes Over Manhattan (ca. 1937) suggests the men huddled around a fire in Isac Friedlander's *Warming Up* have heard that snow has been forecast and are trudging to line up for a snow shovelling job. Often hundreds of men waited all night hoping to be among those selected to clear sidewalks and factory entrances. Like many printmakers of the thirties, Sharp concentrated less on formal problems in favor of communicating themes dictated by social conscience.

Too often critically assessed as naive expressions created solely for the level of perception of the general public, prints of the thirties with social realist content have not been considered major contributions to the development of American art. However, some themes explored by means of graphic media by artists employed by the Federal Art Project have endured as important content in art of the 1960's and 70's, particularly with respect to social and political concerns. The contributions of militant printmakers of the thirties were, unfortunately, eclipsed by the onset of the second World War and, following that, the emergence of Abstract Expressionism which dominated the world of art for nearly two decades. When social comment and printmaking were finally reunited with Pop styles of the 1960's, the depression printmaker was finally accorded a well earned place in the history of American art.

*Snowflakes Over
Manhattan,* ca. 1939
Aquatint
7⅞ x 11⅞ in.

References:
Norman Barr, "Statement," N
York City WPA Art Then
1934–1943 and Now 1960–19
Exhibition Catalog (New Yo
New York City WPA Artists,
Inc., 1977).
Ellen G. Landau, *America In
The War,* Exhibition Catalog
Artists For Victory (Washingto
D.C.: Library of Congress, 19

BENTON SPRUANCE

BENTON SPRUANCE, represented at right with one of his series of four lithographs enigmatically entitled *The People Work* (1937) realized his preference for lithography in 1928 when, as a student at the Pennsylvania Academy of Fine Art, he was awarded a Cresson scholarship to study in Paris. Along with several other American artists, Spruance discovered lithography in Paris at the studio of Edmond and Jacques Desjobert. Expatriate American artists were attracted to the Atelier Desjobert primarily because of the lithographic printers working there, a workshop opportunity not available in the United States. When Spruance noticed that most of the other American artists at the Atelier Desjobert had difficulty communicating with their French printers, he offered to act as interpreter in return for unlimited use of the workshop.[1] Returning to Philadelphia, Spruance associated himself with Theodore Cuno, a superior German lithographer, much in demand by other artists, and who had printed for Joseph Pennell.[2]

Echoing the philosophy of the Federal Art Project, Spruance agreed that ". . .the lithograph is a democratic form of medium. In a democracy, works of art should be available to people in all income brackets. Lithographs can be dispersed among more people at much lower cost than original paintings."[3] Consistent with this view, the work Spruance did between 1935 and the early 1940's reflect a search within his immediate environment for themes which would effectively communicate with a wide and diverse audience. In his introductory notes for *The People Work* portfolio in 1937, Henri Marceau, curator of what is now the Philadelphia Museum of Art, observed that the four lithographs constitute "one artist's saga of the daily toil of his unknown fellow citizens." This toil, Marceau said, as a subject is so much a part of our shared experience that the narrow view sees a sermon, an interpretation that falls short of the full expressive potential of these prints.

In fact, Spruance's people do not work. They are engaged in travelling either to or from their implied labors, relaxing at mid-day and, finally, playing at night. However, a sarcastic intention is unlikely; rather the artist has demonstrated a continuing interest in observing crowds of people.[4] *Morning* examines the mass confusion of a hurrying throng rushing down subway steps and crowding into cars presumably on their way to work. *Noon* crowds people into the street, lunching, gossiping, relaxing and carefully watching the time. *Evening* brings the workers out of their factories and offices to buy newspapers and again swarm into the crush of people in subway stations as they go home. *Night* brings them together again for entertainment, gathering in bars, eating and playing. Work is the implicit theme, but instead of an explicit statement, Spruance has chosen to comment on how work organizes the day. The complexity of the city is generalized into carefully arranged spatial patterns and a generalized humanity.

The People Work (Noon), 1937
Lithograph
Edition 40
13⅝ x 19⅞ in.
Black ink
b.s. lower right
Printed by Cuno

[1] Clinton Adams, *American Lithographers, 1900–1960.* (Albuquerque: University of New Mexico Press, 1983), p.

[2] *The Prints of Benton Murdoc Spruance, A Catalog Raisonné* (Philadelphia: University of Pennsylvania Press, 1986), from intro. by Ruth E. Fine

[3] "Famed Artist Backs Lithos Medium of Democracy," *Germantown Courier* (Germantown, Pennsylvania). 5 March 1958.

[4] *New York Sun* (New York). 10 February 1940.

BERNARD STEFFEN

KANSAS-BORN Bernard Steffen studied art with such distinguished teachers and painters as Stanton MacDonald Wright, Ernest Lawson, Boardman Robinson, and with Thomas Hart Benton at the Kansas City Art Institute. It was apparently while studying with Benton that Steffen's style and preference for rural subject matter evolved. He was a member of the American Artist's Congress, a group established in New York City in 1935 to "endorse government support for art unions and to promote a social-realist style in American painting."[1] He worked as a staff artist for the Resettlement Administration, and painted murals for the WPA, including one for the United States Post Office in Neodesha, Kansas. He was a teacher and treasurer for the National Serigraph Society, and worked comfortably in the varied mediums of oil, tempera, lithography and screen printing.

The strong influence of Benton's style on Steffen's work is evidenced in the work reproduced at the right. Both people and animals are represented with organic shapes, and there is a distinct rhythmic aspect to his work.[2] In these respects his print is similar to *Stacking Hay,* also in this exhibition, a lithograph by Jackson Pollock, who was another Benton student. Steffen's figures, like Pollock's, are broad and simplified, intended as representations of types rather than individuals. Steffen's work, however, lacks the uneasy quality of Pollock's print, perhaps because Steffen was sympathetically drawn to the rural workers who appear in his prints and paintings of the thirties, and he frequently emphasized agricultural themes. Steffen's subject matter, however, does not derive entirely from Benton's influence, but also from his own experiences while growing up in Kansas. His farmers plow, plant and harvest, forming convincing images of rural laborers who made middle America the bread-basket of the world.

Steffen also studied with Stanton McDonald Wright, the American modernist painter who, by 1907, had developed a unique form of abstraction which was inspired by the insistent American assertion of an original visual expression. Wright, along with Morgan Russell and Patrick Henry Bruce, were the only American artists to define a common aesthetic philosophy and issue a manifesto.[3] Evidence of the qualities of Wright's style is seen in Steffen's emphasis on underlying compositional structure.

In *Haying Time* (1941), the figures of the two farmers are nearly engulfed by the results of their labors, an indication of renewed fertility following the ravages of the great drought. The hay rolls down and around them like a great wave. It is not too difficult to believe that Steffen, the cultural worker, may have identified particularly with the men in this print who are also working within the constraints imposed by their environment. Like other artists of the thirties, Steffen's images may be visual confirmation of the link between artist and worker.

Haying Time, 1941
Serigraph
16 x 11 in.

[1] Peter Hastings Falk, ed., *W Was Who in American Art* (Madison, CT: Sound Vie Press, 1985), p. 593.

[2] *Art Digest,* XII (Oct. 1937):

[3] H.H. Arnason, *The Histor Modern Art* (New York: H N. Abrams, Inc. 1986), p.

EDWARD ARTHUR WILSON

BORN IN GLASGOW, SCOTLAND, Edward Arthur Wilson emigrated to the United States in 1893. He studied at the Art Institute of Chicago where he was confronted with, and influenced by, the dominant pioneering industrialism of the time. Wilson's democratic attitudes about the nature and purpose of art, as well as his rigorous self-disciplined approach to his craft, was particularly appropriate during the 1930's when artists were generally defined as cultural workers with aims similar to those of industrial workers.

Primarily an illustrator, Edward Arthur Wilson preferred to have his images reach a large audience through prints rather than to rely upon painted canvases which would be seen by a limited segment of the public. Wilson regarded illustration as an important and challenging aspect of the arts, convinced that all painting necessarily includes a large illustrative component. He earned a reputation for excellence in creating the most salient and original visual interpretations of such literary themes as *Iron Men and Wooden Ships, Two Years Before the Mast, A Man Without A Country,* and *The Ancient Mariner,* among others.

Like the major regionalist artists, including Grant Wood, John Steuart Curry and Thomas Hart Benton, Wilson was not in sympathy with modernist movements which were, in his view, not suited to illustration. Apparently he was neither temperamental nor eccentric, but directed his artistic imagination toward straightforward depictions of gritty themes of both labor and adventure. The decorative and the non-representational did not seem to him to be consistent with his sense of clear, simple narrative which could support itself without reliance upon artifice![1]

Laying Pipe (ca. 1941) was commissioned by the United States Pipe and Steel Foundry Company, and was reproduced in the December 1941 issue of *The U.S. Piper,* their company publication. It pictures a supply line of large diameter cast iron pipe in the process of construction. The burly man with gloved hands who is pouring cement over the joints of the pipe to create a strong seal is being observed by a co-worker who reaches a tatooed arm toward a tool box. Two men in the immediate background are positioning another section of pipe while a third section is held by the large crane above waiting for its placement in the pipeline.

It was the practice of the United States Pipe and Foundry Company to commission an artist for a period of two to three years to illustrate their publication. Wilson, with his experience as illustrator for other publications and a reputation for forceful representations of resolute working men, was an obvious happy choice and remained on their payroll until 1946![2]

Untitled (Laying Pipe), ca. 1941
Lithograph
9˝ x 11⅞ in.

[1] *The Book of Edward A. Wilso A Survey of His Work,* ed. Norman Kent, with a forewo by Thomas Craven (New Yo The Heritage Press, 1948), p. x
[2] *The U.S. Piper,* XIV, No. 4, December, 1941.

GRANT WOOD

PRINTMAKING, FOR GRANT WOOD, was confined to lithography, and repeated themes often better developed in his paintings. He began making lithographs in 1937, completing a total of about twenty during his lifetime.[1] Convinced that each section of the United States was unique in its physiography, industry and local talent, Wood was an important part of the regionalist movement. Thomas Craven, the major critical spokesman for regionalism, identified the movement as a long awaited native expression with a legitimate national theme, declaring: ". . .there is not a self-respecting artist in the country who is not eager to contribute to a movement which has gained the sympathies and support of the American public."[2] Unfortunately, the pressure to appeal to an aesthetically naive public encouraged the production of prints which could be sold for prices as low as five dollars. Wood's lithographs, like those of Thomas Hart Benton and John Steuart Curry, were often produced in large editions and sold by mail order and local department stores.[3]

December Afternoon, 1938, is typical of the homespun, realistic themes which were most successful as prints for the popular taste. It is interesting to note that, in these prints intended for mass distribution, there is little evidence of the irony which makes both *American Gothic,* 1930, and *Daughters of the American Revolution,* 1932, more relevant regionalist statements. The popular prints seem to be concessions to the dictates of regional committees who freely suggested to artists that benign themes would be most appropriate, and who favored historical subjects and nostalgic scenes of familiar rural experience. Wood, like Benton and Curry, repeatedly proclaimed the popular myth of agrarian American values as effective resistance to the threat of internationalism in art. Prints particularly were seen by regionalist artists as the most efficient way to convey the message of rejection of European and American modernist influences to a public which was known to respond favorably to simply rendered, familiar images. Regionalism had no tolerance for innovative directions, including abstraction. It was an affirmation of a conventional preference for realistic representation of themes based on democratic ideals upon which the United States had been founded. Wood, however, chose to simplify forms in the manner of folk art and European primitives, making it even more accessible to rural audiences. The edition of 250 impressions of *December Afternoon* identifies it as one of the prints popularized and published by the Associated American Artists during the thirties, and successfully marketed in major department stores across the country.

December Afternoon, 1941
Lithograph
8⅞ x 11⅞ in.
Edition 250

[1] Una E. Johnson, *American Prints and Printmakers* (New York: Doubleday and Compa Inc., 1980), p. 66.
[2] Clinton Adams, *American Lithographers, 1900–1960* (Albuquerque: The Univers of New Mexico Press, 1983), p. 131.
[3] Adams, p. 140.

Opposite page:

Wood engraving detail from

CLARE LEIGHTON
Plowing, 1932

LOU BARLOW
(1908–)

Tenant Farmers, 1936
WPA Woodcut
7⅞ x 10⅞ in.

T.H. BENTON
(1889–1975)

Cradling Wheat, 1939
Lithograph
9⅝ x 12 in.

Ed. 250. Circulated by Associated American Artists, New York City. Based on the painting *Cradling Wheat* (1938), in the City Art Museum of St. Louis, St. Louis, Missouri.

The Woodpile, 1939
Lithograph 8¾ x 10⅞ in.

Circulated by Associated American Artists, New York City. Study for a small painting done in 1940, present location unknown.

HENRY BILLINGS
(1901–)

Men and Machines, 1931
Lithograph
14 x 16 in.

Men and Machines, 1931
Lithograph
14 x 17 in.

Men and Machines, 1931
Lithograph
15¾ x 13¾ in.

Men and Machines, 1931
Lithograph
15 x 13¾ in.

Men and Machines, 1931
Lithograph
15¾ x 13¾ in.

JOHN STEUART CURRY
(1897–1946)

Prize Stallions, 1938
Lithograph
12¾ x 8¾ in.

Ed. 250. Circulated by Associated American Artists. Initialed and dated in stone, l.l.

ISAC FRIEDLANDER
(1890–)

Warming Up, ca. 1935
Etching
9¾ x 11⅞ in.

LEON GILMOUR
(1907–)

Cement Finishers, 1939
Wood Engraving
10⅛ x 8⅛ in.

HARRY GOTTLIEB
(1895–)

Change of Shift, 1940
WPA Serigraph
16¾ x 20 in.

Going to Work, 1941
WPA Serigraph
15 x 20 in.

IRWIN HOFFMAN
(1901–)

Miner at Rest, 1937
Etching
9¾ x 7⅞ in.
Cigarette Underground, 1938
Etching
10¾ x 8¹⁵⁄₁₆ in.
Signed in pencil.

JOE JONES
(1909–1963)

Untitled (Harvest Workers), ca. 1940
Lithograph
9⅞ x 8 in.

CHET LA MORE
(1908–)

Untitled (Furnace), 1936
WPA Lithograph
12 x 14⅞ in.
Signed in pencil.
Untitled (Auto Worker), 1937
WPA Lithograph
11¾ x 19 in.

PAUL LANDACRE
(1893–1963)

Poachers, 1934
Wood Engraving
6 x 7½ in.
Signed and dated in pencil.
Amateurs, 1937
Wood Engraving
7 x 11 in.

CLARE LEIGHTON
(1900–)

Cutting, 1931
Wood Engraving
8 x 11¼ in.
Lumber camp series. Hardie, 199. Signed in pencil.
Loading, 1931
Wood Engraving
11¾ x 8¾ in.
Lumber camp series. Hardie, 198. Signed in pencil.
Cider Making, 1932
Wood Engraving
8½ x 10 in.
Plowing, 1932
Wood Engraving
7⅜ x 9¹³⁄₁₆ in.
Sheep Shearing, 1932
Wood Engraving
7⅞ x 10 ¼ in.
Apple Picking, 1933
Wood Engraving
7⅞ x 8⅝ in.

HERSCHEL LEVIT
(1912–)

Dam Builders, 1937
Lithograph
9¼ x 12¼ in.

Take It Away, 1940
Lithograph
9¾ x 13½ in.

LOUIS LOZOWICK
(1892–1973)

Construction (Excavation), 1930
Lithograph
15¹⁵⁄₁₆ x 6⁵⁄₁₆ in.
Ed. 25. Printed by George C. Miller. Plate
cancelled.

Mid-Air, 1931
Lithograph
11⁷⁄₁₆ x 6½ in.
Ed. 50.

*Through Brooklyn Bridge Cables (Bridge
Repairs, Repairing Brooklyn Bridge)*, 1938
Lithograph
9⁵⁄₈ x 12¹³⁄₁₆ in.
Ed. 15. Printed 1939 for Associated American
Artists in an edition of 250; printed by
George C. Miller.

Birth of a Skyscraper, 1939
Lithograph
12³⁄₁₆ x 8⁵⁄₈ in.
Ed. 25.

Derricks and Men (Riding the Girder), 1939
Lithograph
12¹⁵⁄₁₆ x 8½ in.
Ed. 15. Printed by George C. Miller.

*Granite for Monuments (For Future
Monuments)*, 1939
Lithograph
12¹⁵⁄₁₆ x 8½ in.
Ed. 15. Printed by George C. Miller.

Guts of Manhattan, 1939
Lithograph
13³⁄₁₆ x 9¼ in.
Ed. 20. Printed by George C. Miller. Done while
subway lines were under construction along
Sixth and Eighth avenues, at the same time as
the Sixth avenue elevated was being demolished.

S.L. MARGOLIES
(1898–)

Builders of Babylon, 1937
Etching/Aquatint
14¼ x 11 in.

REGINALD MARSH (1898–1954)	*Chop Suey Dancers*, 1930 Etching and Engraving 7⅞ x 5⅞ in. State 5, Final State. Printing: Marsh, impr. 1–14 Whatman. *Modern 1939 Venus*, 1939 Etching 7⅞ x 11¾ in. State V, Final State. Printing: Marsh, 10: 5 Whatman, 5 Rives (Sept. 28, 1939). Edition: Whitney, 100 impr. (1969). *Merry Go Round*, 1940 Engraving 7⅞ x 11⅞ in. State I of III. Edition: Whitney 100 impr. (1969).
JACKSON POLLOCK (1912–1956)	*Stacking Hay*, ca. 1935–36 Lithograph 9⅜ x 13 in.
WILLIAM SHARP (1900–1961)	*Chicago Steel Mills*, ca. 1937 Aquatint 10⅞ x 8¾ in. *Railroad Yards*, ca. 1937 Aquatint 10½ x 9⅜ in. *Snowflakes over Manhattan*, ca. 1939 Aquatint 7⅞ x 11⅞ in.
BENTON SPRUANCE (1904–1967)	*The People Work, Morning*, 1937 Lithograph 19 x 13¾ in. 27/40 *The People Work, Noon*, 1937 Lithograph 19 x 13¾ in. 27/40 *The People Work, Evening*, 1937 Lithograph 19 x 13¾ in. *The People Work, Night*, 1937 Lithograph 19 x 13¾ in.
BERNARD STEFFEN (1907–197?)	*Haying Time*, 1941 Serigraph 16 x 11 in. *Spring*, ca. 1941 Serigraph 12¹¹⁄₁₆ x 9⅝ in.

EDWARD ARTHUR WILSON *Untitled (Laying Pipe)*, 1941
(1886–1970)   Lithograph
                                        13½ x 8½ in.

GRANT WOOD   *December Afternoon*, 1938
(1891–1942)   Lithograph
                                        9 x 11⅞ in.
                                        Fertility, 1939
                                        Lithograph
                                        9 x 11⅞ in.
                                        Ed. 250. Published by Associated American
                                        Artists, New York. Signed in pencil, l.r.

SELECTED BIBLIOGRAPHY

Adams, Clinton. *American Lithographers 1900–1940*. Albuquerque, New Mexico: University of New Mexico Press, 1983: pp. 50–71.

Alloway, Lawrence. "The Recovery of Regionalism: John Steuart Curry." *Art in America* 64 (July 1976): pp. 70–73.

————. "Isabel Bishop, the Grand Manner and the Working Girl." *Art in America* 63 (Sept./Oct. 1975): pp. 61–65.

Beall, Karen F. *American Prints in the Library of Congress, A Catalog of the Collection*. Baltimore, Maryland: The Johns Hopkins Press, 1970.

Bean, Walton. *California, An Interpretive History*. New York: McGraw-Hill, 1968.

Barlow, Louis. Interview with artist, January 22, 1988.

Bloxom, Marguerite D. *Pickaxe and Pencil, References for the Study of the WPA*. Washington, D.C.: Library of Congress, 1982.

"Clare Leighton Wood Engravings." Exhibition Catalog, Associated American Artists, Sept. 19–Oct. 8, 1983.

Cohen, Marilyn. *Reginald Marsh's New York*. New York: Dover Publications, 1983.

Cole, Sylvan, Jr. *The Lithographs of John Steuart Curry*. New York: Associated American Artists, 1976.

"Contemporary Art Presents Steffen, Kansan." *Art Digest* XII (October 1, 1937): p. 15.

Contreras, Belisario. *Tradition and Innovation in New Deal Art*. New Jersey: Associated University Press, 1983.

Corn, Wanda. *Grant Wood: The Regionalist Vision*. New Haven: Yale University Press, 1983.

Czestochowski, Joseph S. *John Steuart Curry and Grant Wood: A Portrait of Rural America*. Columbia, MO: University of Missouri Press, 1981.

————. "John Steuart Curry's Lithographs—A Portrait of Rural America." *American Art Journal* IX (November 1977): pp. 68–82.

Dennis, James M. *Grant Wood: A Study in American Art and Culture*, 2nd ed. Columbia, MO: Missouri University Press, 1986.

Egbert, Donald Drew. *Socialism and American Art*. Princeton, NJ: Princeton University Press, 1967.

Evans, J. Warren, Anthony Borton, Harold F. Hintz and L. Dale Van Vleck. *The Horse*. San Francisco: W.H. Freeman, 1977.

Fath, Creekmore, ed. *The Lithographs of Thomas Hart Benton*. Austin, TX: University of Texas Press, 1969.

Flint, Janet. *The Prints of Louis Lozowick*. New York: Hudson Hills Press, 1982.

Francey, Mary. *Joseph Pennell, Illustrator and Printmaker, 1857–1926*. University of Utah, 1974.

Friedlander, Isac. Archives of American Art, Roll 89.

Garraty, John. *The Great Depression*. New York: Harcourt Brace Jovanovich, 1986.

Goodrich, Lloyd. "Reginald Marsh: Painter of New York in its Wildest Profusion." *American Artist* 19 (Sept. 1955): pp. 18–23, 61–63.

Gottlieb, Harry. Interview with artist, January 29, 1988.

———. Archives of American Art, Roll DC/113, Frames 290–397; Roll D343, Frames 143–148; Roll N69/82, Frames 464–467, 480–481.

Grenauer, Emily. "WPA Influences." *New York City WPA Art Then 1934–1943 and Now 1960–1977.* New York: WPA Artists, Inc., 1974.

Haines, Francis. *Horses in America.* New York: Thomas Y. Crowell Co., 1971.

Hardie, Martin. *"The Wood Engravings of Clare Leighton."* Print Collectors Quarterly 22 (April 1935): pp. 139–165.

Heller, N. and J. Williams. "John Steuart Curry: The American Farmlands." *American Artist* 40 (January 1976): pp. 46–51, 96.

"John Steuart Curry". Exhibition Catalog. Kansas: Kansas University Press, 1970.

Johnson, Una E. *American Prints and Printmakers.* Garden City, NY: Doubleday and Company, Inc., 1980.

Kainen, Jacob. "Prints of the Thirties: Reflections on the Federal Art Project." *Artists Proof* 11 (1971): pp. 34–41.

Kendall, M. Sue. *Re-thinking Regionalism: John Steuart Curry and the Kansas Mural Controversy.* Washington, D.C.: Smithsonian Institution Press, 1986.

Laning, Edward. "Through the Eyes of Marsh." *Art News* 54 (Sept. 1955): pp. 22–24.

Larsen, Susan C. "The American Abstract Artists: A Documentary History, 1936–1941." *Archives of American Art Journal* 14, No. 1 (1974): pp. 1–6.

LaMore, Chet. Archives of American Art, Roll 1088.

Lavender, David. *California.* New York: W.W. Norton, 1976.

Leighton, Clare. "How I Made My Book." *American Artist* 19 (Feb. 1955): pp. 40–45.

Marling, Karal Ann. *Wall-to-Wall America.* Minneapolis, MN: University of Minnesota Press, 1982.

McCreery, Margaret. "The Woodcuts of Paul Landacre." *Print Connoisseur* 1 (1932): pp. 120–131.

McDonald, William F. *Federal Relief Administration and the Arts.* Columbus, OH: Ohio State University Press, 1969.

Millier, Arthur. "Paul Landacre, Wood Engraver." *Prints* 1 (1931): pp. 42–45.

Monroe, Gerald M. "Artists as Militant Trade Union Workers During the Great Depression." *Archives of American Art Journal* 14, No. 1 (1974): pp. 7–10.

———. "Art Front." *Archives of American Art Journal* 13, No. 3 (1973): pp. 13–19.

"New Horizons in American Art." New York, 1935. Introduction by Holger Cahill.

O'Connor, Francis V. *Art for the Millions*. Greenwich, CT: New York Graphic Society, Ltd. 1973: pp. 139–141, 154–156.

_____. *Federal Support for the Visual Arts: The New Deal Then and Now*. Greenwich, CT: New York Graphic Society, Ltd., 1969.

Olds, Elizabeth. "Prints for Mass Production." *Art for the Millions*, ed. Francis V. O'Connor. Greenwich, CT: New York Graphic Society, Ltd., 1973: pp. 142–144.

"Paul Landacre Association." Archives of American Art, American Artists Group, Inc. Roll N/AG-11, Frames 361–364.

Prints of Benton Murdoch Spruance. Philadelphia: University of Pennsylvania Press, 1986. Introduction by Ruth E. Fine.

Published Plates of Irwin D. Hoffman. New York: Associated American Artists, 1936. Introduction by Margaret Sullivan.

Reese, Albert. *American Prize Prints of the 20th Century*. New York: American Artists Group, Inc., 1949.

Sasowsky, Norman. *The Prints of Reginald Marsh*. New York: Clarkson N. Potter, Publ., 1976.

Schmeckebier, Laurence E. *John Steuart Curry's Pageant of America*. New York: American Artists Group, 1943.

Slatkin, Wendy. *Women Artists in History*. New Jersey: Prentice-Hall, Inc., 1985: pp. 114–116.

Steffen, Bernard. Archives of American Art, Roll N108, Frames 723–724; Roll DC114, Frames 931–933.

Taylor, Joshua. *America As Art*. Washington, D.C.: Smithsonian Institution Press, 1976.

_____. "A Poignant, Relevant Backward Look at Artists of the Great Depression." *Smithsonian* 10, No. 7 (Oct. 1979): pp. 44–53.

Vincent, Sybil. "In the Studio of Clare Leighton." *London Studio* 13 (1937): pp. 144–147.

Wiley, John, Jr. "Phenomena, Comment and Notes." *Smithsonian* 18, No. 11 (1988): pp. 38–42.

Zigrosser, Carl. *The Artist in America: Twenty-Four Close-Ups of Contemporary Printmakers*. New York: Alfred A. Knopf, 1942.

83

1,400 copies of
DEPRESSION
PRINTMAKERS
AS WORKERS
were printed in
April, 1988.
The papers are
French's Speckletone
Cream Text and
Chipboard Text, and
Monadnock's Caress
Cover and 80 lb. Smooth Text.
Typefaces used were
Futura Condensed Medium and Bold
and Goudy Oldstyle Book and Italic.
Graphic Designer • Scott Mooy
Photographer • Joseph Marotta
Typesetter • Whipple & Associates
Printer • Quality Press
Paper • Unisource and Zellerbach
All of Salt Lake City, Utah.